CONSPIRACY

CONSPIRACY

*The Implications
of the Harrisburg Trial
for the Democratic
Tradition*

edited by
John C. Raines

HARPER & ROW, Publisher

New York, Evanston, San Francisco, London

Designed by Gwendolyn O. England

Library of Congress Cataloging in Publication Data
Main entry under title:

Conspiracy; the implications of the Harrisburg trial
   for the democratic tradition.
   Includes bibliographical references.
   1. Harrisburg Seven (Trial) 2. United States—
Politics and government—1969–   I. Raines, John C.,
ed.
KF224.H27C65   345′.73′0231   72–78066
ISBN 0–06–066772–9

Contents

Preface

ON A COLD NOVEMBER DAY in 1969, the first antiwar march assembled on the grounds of the Washington Monument. Across the ellipse, a line of buses, bumper to bumper, could be seen ringing the White House. Inside, the President watched a football game on TV. It's a revealing scene of the pervasive mood of embattlement that gripped the upper echelons of White House power during those years. Convinced of its political virtue but less than sure in 1970 of its political majority, the administration went on the counterattack. Its chief instrument was America's need to believe in itself.

It was not, however, a happy time to secure the dignity of authority. The campuses, the ghettos and the stock market were all in disarray. The old Protestant denominations—or at least their leaders—were in open revolt against the war. Even the Catholic bishops, so long a dependable support of God and country, were visibly less than pleased. Only Billy Graham in a sign of things to come continued to pack in audiences with the old nostalgia. The task of pacifying dissent and returning politics to the professionals had clearly to be high on any political agenda unprepared to accept fundamental change in America. A White House which felt itself assaulted by its moral critics was determined to strike back in kind.

Men of experienced power have known all along that our country is thoroughly hooked upon the purity of its morality, prepared to be cynical about its politicians but not about its wars. The Calley affair showed that. No, we simply have to take former Vice President Agnew at his word when he said of Vietnam: "It will be remembered as our most moral war." The issue was fundamental. The war (implicating as well its prosecutors) was either a moral crusade or a disaster. For authority and respect to be confidently rehabiliated the dissenters had to be driven not just into silence but into moral humiliation. As former White House chief-of-staff "Bob" Haldeman penned alongside a notice of possible obscene language to be used against the President by protestors at a Billy Graham rally, "Great!"

A variety of both legal and extralegal weapons were available in the task of morally undermining the administration's moral critics. Many of the former were first developed in the Kennedy Justice Department to attack organized crime. Yet once in law they could be targeted for purposes not originally intended by Congress. Laws, like wars, have a way of getting out of hand. Concerning the extralegal devices of attack, the Watergate investigations have shown the Nixon administration to possess a peculiar genius of its own.

Given the task of renovating a tarnished moral reputation, conspiracy indictments became an administrative favorite to blunt peace movement criticism and redirect its energies inward to self-defense and the paying of overwhelming legal costs—over a half million dollars at Harrisburg.

Conspiracy is a sinister word. It conjures up memories of organized crime and Nazi saboteurs. For most citizens, it names the dividing line between decent people and the underworld of the desperate, the clandestine, and the violent. We tend to forget that conspiracy laws first became widely used in the 1920s to break up organized labor. In the sixties this reversal of the direction of moral accusation proved an effective way of keeping most decent folk if not quite satisfied, then at least off-balance.

Now the sad truth is that all this worked pretty well. The movement was ill-prepared for the politics of courtroom exhaustion. Even less prepared was it for the interpersonal subversion and spreading network of suspicion caused by the massive influx of government informers. We will want to examine both of these potent weapons in the pages that follow. Still, why were the resisters such easy targets? Were they crippled by a contempt toward everyday American reality, on an ego trip incapable of disciplining itself to maximum political effect? True, jury after jury refused to convict. But without the accident of the Watergate scandal, this silencing of domestic dissent would have remained a mute witness to successful citizen pacification—a bad lesson to leave on the national record. Could the Berrigans have done better at avoiding it?

Politics, law, but perhaps especially the struggle for moral justification are the subjects of this book. An attempt has been made to probe the issues which remain behind after the court-room empties and the sometimes dramatic and sometimes simply bizarre deciphering of innocence and guilt is past. The Berrigan conspiracy trial remains noteworthy, finally, not because of the wisdom or virtue, or the lack thereof, in the contending parties, but because much that we need to know better about ourselves as a people was brought into sharp focus there.

We are a diverse group of authors assembled for this task, with strong and diverse perceptions. We have tried not to talk past each other—so easy these days—but to construct a conversation. We met with each other for many hours both before and after the trial. For that seriousness of effort, the editor thanks his col-leagues and believes you will want to also. Harper & Row facili-tated these conversations, and took a long bet on a late contender in a field already saturated with comment. Teri Simon helped dig out the trial transcript and so helped get at the truth. Dean Kelley paid for its photocopying. The book belongs in part to all of them.

John C. Raines

Glen Lake, Michigan, 1973

We ask our fellow citizens to match our lives, our actions, against the actions of the president, his advisers, his chiefs of staff, and we pose the question: Who has committed the crimes of violence?

—Statement of the Harrisburg defendants at the time of their indictment

Furthermore, the witness said, there had been "a certain atmosphere" in the White House, a feeling that, if the dissenters could break the law, the President's defenders could reply in kind. . . . "Although I was aware they were illegal and I am sure the others did, we had become somewhat inured to using some activities that would help us in accomplishing what we thought was a cause, a legitimate cause."

—Jeb Magruder at the Watergate Hearings, in the *New York Times,* June 15, 1973

Introduction

ROBERT MCAFEE BROWN

THE LONDON VISITOR who searches in St. Paul's Church for a
monument to its architect, Christopher Wren, will discover an old
Latin motto describing the true state of affairs: *Si monumentum
requiriis circumspice* (If you wish a monument, look about you).
In recent times, when the traffic patterns outside St. Paul's have
made human survival there a precarious matter, one of the deans
of St. Paul's has suggested placing another Latin motto above the
main exit door: *Nisi monumentum requiriis circumspice* (Unless
you wish a monument, look about you).

When this book was initially undertaken, the dean's advice
could have served as a summary description of the lessons of the
Harrisburg trial: America, unless you wish a monument, record-
ing your demise, look carefully at what is happening about you,
and take the necessary corrective measures. You are moving
toward a police state, in which high government officials can
make sensationalistic and unsubstantiated charges against their
opponents, in which high government officials will hire convicted
criminals to spy and lie for them, in which high government
officials are willing to prostitute the judicial process for legislative
gain, in which high government officials in whom we should be
able to repose trust will do wrong and call it right, all in the name
of "national security."

To have spoken that way even a year ago would have gained
credence only among the already convinced, and would have

Robert McAfee Brown is a well-known peace activist and professor of
religion at Stanford University. He is author of numerous books and
articles, including *Vietnam: Crisis of Conscience* and *Pseudonyms of God.*

seemed to most sober persons to be an extravagant extrapolation from the insufficient evidence of one relatively tiny incident.

No more. For in the interval, the Watergate scandal has broken wide open, and from one bungled burglary has escalated into the most chilling revelation of corruption in high places that American history has yet experienced. We have learned in the interval that the government's duplicity in events relating to the Harrisburg trial was not an isolated instance but was part of a grand design of officially engineered deception that has brought down many of the employees of the White House and has irrevocably tarnished the administration of its most illustrious inhabitant. We now know, whatever further revelations may come, that the police state mentality so apparent in the events surrounding the Harrisburg trial was not only condoned by the White House but was actually fostered by it, and, more frightening still, has been unambiguously justified by the chief actors involved. To our numbed amazement, we have discovered that illegal bugging, falsification of official documents, burglary, deliberate deception by White House spokesmen and inhabitants were all part of the "game plan" and have all been piously and self-righteously defended in the interests of "national security" and "loyalty to the President"—two goals that turn out in the minds of their proponents to be mutually interchangeable.

The most outlandish perversions of the democratic process that could have been conjured up in our imaginations now turn out to be mere descriptions of the actions and rationale of those closest to the President himself. In a supreme irony, those who have publicly preached "law and order" turn out to be those who have most surreptitiously practiced illegality and disorder.

The magnitude of this betrayal of public trust by the White House, far from minimizing the importance of a careful analysis of the Harrisburg trial, serves rather to accentuate its importance, for in the Harrisburg trial we see the proponents of "law and order" in their public posture of self-righteousness, some time before their private posture of hypocrisy was revealed for all to see. It has been a temptation to tell the story of the Harrisburg trial in the light of the subsequent Watergate exposures, but it is a temptation that (for the most part) has been resisted. Watergate italicizes the importance of Harrisburg but it should not engulf it, for the Harrisburg story needs telling on its own terms. It shows us a nation inching toward fascism, and if that process is now being reversed, it will be only because the eternal vigilance of which Thomas Jefferson spoke remains continually focused on events like Harrisburg and Watergate and presidential lies about Cambodia. The lessons of Harrisburg are crucial lessons for the recovery of health in our democratic process. *Nisi monumentum requiriis circumspice.*

On November 27, 1970—a day that may not live in infamy but will remain one of the more tarnished days in recent American history—J. Edgar Hoover appeared before the Senate Appropriations Subcommittee to ask for an increase of $14,000,000 in funding for the FBI, so that he could hire 1,000 new agents and 702 new clerks. As an illustration of the need for more resources to combat crime, he announced to the subcommittee that Philip and Daniel Berrigan were the "principal leaders" of a group that "plans to blow up underground electrical conduits and steam pipes serving the Washington, D.C. area in order to disrupt federal government operations" and that was "concocting a scheme to kidnap a highly placed government official."[1] Although the subcommittee was meeting in closed session, Mr. Hoover provided mimeographed copies of his remarks for the press.

Sensation. Sensation on at least three counts: (a) Mr. Hoover did not document his charges, although it is the usual practice in a democracy for law-enforcement officials to couple charges with evidence; (b) since Philip and Daniel Berrigan had both been in jail for months, it was difficult to understand how they could be masterminding such a plot; and (c) both of them were known to be deeply committed pacifists whose principles would clearly preclude carrying out the activities with which they were charged.

Nevertheless, the charges had been made, and they were serious. The next day, through their lawyers, the Berrigans insisted that Mr. Hoover either fish or cut bait: "We have already been tried and condemned by Mr. Hoover's remarks, and we should have an equal opportunity to answer his charge. He ought, in view of the seriousness of the allegations he has made, either to prosecute us or publicly retract the charges he has made."

ESCALATION: MILITARY AND MORAL

How could things have come to such a pass? How could the issues have been joined in such apparently bizarre fashion? A backward look will help to position both the episode and its aftermath.

By the time Lyndon Johnson became president in 1963, it was clear that both the Eisenhower and Kennedy administrations had been making increasing military commitments in Vietnam. In the 1964 presidential campaign, Vietnam was a major issue, and despite Mr. Johnson's pledge that if re-elected he would not escalate the war, he was re-elected and he did escalate the war. ("They told me," one disgruntled Republican observed early in 1965, "that if I voted for Goldwater the war would escalate. So I voted for Goldwater and the war escalated.")

Throughout Mr. Johnson's entire second term in office and Mr. Nixon's first term in office, the war continued to escalate. (In the name of "winding down the war" Mr. Nixon has dropped more bombs on Vietnam than his predecessor came close to dropping in the name of widening the war, which means that he has ordered the dropping of more bombs than any other man in human history.) During this period, Johnson, Humphrey and Rusk were scornful of those who protested the war, demeaning their integrity and challenging their patriotism—a tune Nixon, Agnew and Mitchell sang even more stridently after 1968. This was the period of "the credibility gap," the period when extraordinary numbers of Americans made the extraordinary discovery that they could no longer believe what their Presidents

were saying. And all the while, increased thousands of Vietnamese and Americans were dying needless and horrible deaths.

To those within the peace movement first of all, and to ever
greater numbers of other Americans later on, the escalation of
military power demanded the escalation of moral protest. Letters,
speeches, rallies, marches, demonstrations, all were apparently to
no avail; the war got worse. For many, as for the Berrigans, the
moral protest finally crossed the line to nonviolent civil disobedience. Young men refused induction into the armed forces—
and were jailed. Philip Berrigan with a group of friends poured
blood on Baltimore draft records—and was jailed. Subsequently
he and his brother Daniel and seven other Catholic friends
poured napalm on Catonsville draft records—and were jailed,
although Daniel, in the best traditions of early Jesuit history and
to the acute discomfort of the FBI, went underground and eluded
Mr. Hoover's finest for four merry and agonizing months.

Both of the Berrigans, in other words, along with other war
protesters, were gradually "radicalized" both by the enormity of
the slaughter of Vietnamese by Americans, and by the utter
intransigency of both the Johnson and Nixon administrations;
the move from being on the letterhead of "Clergy and Laymen
Concerned About Vietnam" to using napalm against draft records
is no small move. But on one point they and their whole circle of
friends remained consistent: they saw no point in protesting
violence abroad by engaging in violence at home; they were not
about to promote international peace by waging domestic war.
They were pacifists, in other words, both for pragmatic reasons
and for reasons of principle. One can be a pacifist for either
reason; they were for both. And there were many occasions (such
as the evening "demonstrations" during the time of the Catonsville trial) when it took the combined rhetoric and example of the
Berrigans and their friends to keep "peace" advocates from
crossing the threshold to demonstrations that would have ended
with senseless violence. That Mr. Hoover should accuse such men
of masterminding plots to blow up buildings and kidnap government officials might be consistent with Mr. Hoover's sense of the

appropriate, but it was far from consistent with what either the Berrigans or their supporters would consider morally or pragmatically appropriate.

Enter Congressman William R. Anderson (D., Tenn.), naval hero and former submarine commander, who had visited the Berrigans three times in prison and came to the conclusion that they had "something from which we can all learn." Mr. Hoover made his charges on a Friday. On the following Monday he had a letter from Congressman Anderson:

"The Berrigans have always followed a course of total nonviolence toward their fellow human beings. . . . If there is any substance to your allegations, . . . it is your duty to arraign them before a federal grand jury to seek an indictment. If, on the other hand, there is no substance, or your remarks were misconstrued, then certainly we should expect an explanation, if not an outright retraction."

And then, sensing the more far-reaching implications of Mr. Hoover's action, Congressman Anderson concluded: "It adds to what seems to me a growing tendency on the part of our Executive Branch to employ the tactics of fear and to be less than candid in dealing with the public. . . . Our system of government is endangered when anything less than an open, candid and humble relationship exists between the government and the people."

Receiving only a curt response from Mr. Hoover, Mr. Anderson continued his questioning on the House floor on December 9, accusing Mr. Hoover of "tactics reminiscent of McCarthyism, using newspaper headlines and scare dramatics rather than due process of law. . . ." He asserted categorically that he did not believe the charges, stated that Mr. Hoover's publicizing of such unsubstantiated charges represented an unfortunate erosion of the democratic process, and concluded by saying that either the Berrigans "are dangerous—or there is a still more dangerous plot afoot to repress their political dissent against war and justice." There was little doubt where Congressman Anderson felt the true danger lay.

Vice President Agnew, remaining totally in character, described Congressman Anderson's public defense of the Berrigans as "emotional self-serving claptrap."

NOT ONE INDICTMENT BUT TWO

Not until January 12, 1971—almost seven weeks after Mr. Hoover's sensationalistic charges—did Attorney General John Mitchell announce that a federal grand jury had indicted Philip Berrigan and five others on charges of conspiring both to blow up the heating system of federal buildings in Washington and to kidnap Henry Kissinger. Daniel Berrigan and seven others were cited as "co-conspirators" but not as defendants. Twenty-two "overt acts" were listed, most of them being telephone calls or visits between the defendants. Those indicted were Eqbal Ahmad, Fr. Philip Berrigan, Sr. Elizabeth McAlister, Fr. Neil McLaughlin, Anthony Scoblick and Fr. Joseph Wenderoth. Those cited as "co-conspirators" (a designation that still remains a mystery) were Sr. Beverly Bell, Fr. Daniel Berrigan, William Davidon, Tom Davidson, Sr. Jogues Egan, Fr. Paul Mayer, and Marjorie Shuman.

The indictment was hastily drawn up. Proof that the government itself came to share this estimate is indicated by the fact that a new indictment, to which we will subsequently refer, was later substituted for it. Nor was the public overwhelmed by the workmanship of John Mitchell's craftsmen. The New York *Times* stated that the indictment "is itself almost a conspiracy against sober reason," while the St. Louis *Post-Dispatch* offered the opinion that it "must be one of the flimsiest on record." As reporters analyzed the document, they began to realize the most of the charges were based on information supplied by an FBI "informer" who was possibly an *agent provocateur* as well.

Enter Boyd F. Douglas, Jr. In the annals of the psychology of the criminal mind, books could be written about this man, who operated under any one of fifteen different aliases. Since 1963 Douglas had spent most of his time in federal penitentiaries for a variety of offenses ranging from assaulting an FBI agent to passing more than $60,000 worth of bad checks to impersonating an army officer while trying to defraud the PX at Fort Sam Houston in Texas. Although he never got beyond Texas in his military service (from which he received a dishonorable discharge), he told people he had served in the army in Vietnam; although he was in good health, he told one girl that he had less than a year to live and wanted her to give him a few months of happiness; although he was in the pay of the FBI, he told Philip Berrigan that he was deeply active in the peace movement. It is scarcely surprising that Boyd F. Douglas, Sr. said of his son, "He has told so many lies practically all his life that I can't believe anything he says."

For a man with such a background, Douglas had astonishing freedom at Lewisburg as the only one of 1,400 prisoners permitted to pursue a student-inmate program at nearby Bucknell University. This got him out of prison every day, it got him a pad in town, and (when he became the courier of the smuggled letters between Father Berrigan and Sister Elizabeth) it got him retainer fees from the FBI. To be sure, Douglas was not satisfied with the fees the FBI paid him for betraying his "friends," and toward the end of his period of informing he asked for an extra tax-free $50,000 for his services—which in these inflationary times is perhaps the modern equivalent of twelve pieces of silver—along with a forged good conduct army discharge for use in establishing himself in society after the trial. The government's final financial settlement with Douglas remains enveloped in a cloud of secrecy similar to the one that surrounded him between his "surfacing" and his appearance at the trial fourteen months later.

On February 8, 1971, the six defendants were arraigned in Harrisburg and pleaded "not guilty" to all charges. Along with their "co-conspirators" they issued a public statement sorting out the moral issues they believed were at stake:

We are thirteen men and women who state with clear conscience that we are neither conspirators nor bombers nor kidnapers. In principle and in fact we have rejected all acts such as these of which we have

been accused. We are a diverse group, united by a common goal: our
opposition to the massive violence of our government in its war
against southeast Asia. It is because of this opposition that we have
been branded a conspiracy.

Our anguish for the victims of this brutal war has led all of us to
nonviolent resistance, some of us to the destruction of draft records.
But, unlike the accuser, the government of the United States, we have
not advocated or engaged in violence against human beings. Unlike
the government, we have nothing to hide. We ask our fellow citizens
to match our lives, our actions, against the actions of the President,
his advisers, his chiefs of staff, and we pose the question: who has
committed the crimes of violence?

After being publicly arraigned on one indictment, the defendants were subsequently tried on a second, issued three weeks
later on April 30, 1971. While retaining some sense of continuity
with its predecessor, the new indictment outlined a more intricate
plot and a somewhat different cast of characters. Now there were
eight "conspirators" instead of six: Eqbal Ahmad, Fr. Philip
Berrigan, Theodore Glick (whose case was later severed for
separate trial), Sr. Elizabeth McAlister, Fr. Neil McLaughlin,
Anthony Scoblick, Mary Cain Scoblick and Fr. Joseph Wenderoth. Now there were four "co-conspirators" instead of eight: Sr.
Beverly Bell, William Davidon, Sr. Jogues Egan and Marjorie
Shuman. Daniel Berrigan, who Mr. Hoover had informed the
Senate Appropriations Subcommittee and the world was one of
the two "principal leaders" of the entire action, was no longer
listed even as a "co-conspirator." There were ten counts against
the defendants. The first and most important count charged the
defendants were conspiring (a) to effect a series of raids against
draft boards (a new charge and one that a number of the defendants had earlier and freely confessed to), (b) to blow up the
heating system in various federal buildings in Washington, and
(c) to kidnap Henry Kissinger. A list of thirty-five "overt acts"
was appended to this first count.

The joining of these three alleged acts (raiding, bombing and
kidnaping) in a single charge was an extraordinarily clever

move by the prosecution. *In effect* it defused and even negated
the earlier bombing and kidnaping charges, since in order to
prove conspiracy the government needed only to show that one of
the three acts had been contemplated. Thus, if the defendants
were found guilty only of conspiring to raid draft boards, they
would still be guilty of the first count, even if no evidence were
produced that they had planned to bomb or kidnap. Since the
bombing and kidnaping had been mentioned in Mr. Hoover's
original charges (with not even a whisper about draft board
raids) the clear impression would be left with the public that guilt
on one part meant guilt on all three parts of the charge. It was a
clear case of the whole being equal to considerably less than the
sum of its parts.

Counts II–X charge that letters and packages had been illegally
sent to and from Lewisburg prison by Philip Berrigan, Sr. Elizabeth McAlister and Eqbal Ahmad. Count II includes a long
section of a letter from Sister Elizabeth to Father Berrigan, and
count III includes much of his reply. The portions quoted deal
mainly with the alleged plot to kidnap Henry Kissinger. (Normally such materials would be introduced as evidence during the
trial itself, and the inclusion of the texts in the indictment itself
was, to say the least, unusual. The defense lawyers in fact tried,
unsuccessfully, to argue that the release of the letters in advance
of the trial was prejudicial to their clients.)

These letters were a substantial part of the case presented in
court, and Boyd Douglas's testimony was designed to corroborate
and expand their contents. Sister Elizabeth, apparently trying to
buoy Father Berrigan's spirits about the ongoing vitality of the
peace movement, describes a notion that had emerged out of a
brief discussion at a weekend party, a notion so far out that she
admonishes him not to put anything about it down on paper(!)
or even to mention it to brother Daniel. This notion was the
possibility of a kidnaping or "citizen's arrest" of Henry Kissinger, after which he would be confronted with political liberals
(likewise kidnaped and with stockings over their faces) who
would discuss the war with him and try to get political conces-

sions from him as the basis for his release. The matter had indeed been raised in discussion and then apparently forgotten. As Francine du Plessix Gray reports it, "Elizabeth put a magnifying glass on a twenty-minute discussion of a citizen's arrest."[2] Father Berrigan's reply was a combination of admiration and a few put downs, along with the suggestion of "weaving some elements of modesty" into the scheme.

The proposal is so fanciful, and from any realistic point of view so impractical and implausible, that it is hard to understand how it was taken seriously by the government. Indeed, it is clear that not even the FBI took it seriously at first, since its surveillance of Sister Elizabeth had been for the purpose of tracking down the then-hidden Daniel Berrigan. When hints from her letters did in fact lead the FBI to Block Island and the capture of the Jesuit fugitive, surveillance of Sr. Elizabeth was discontinued, and not resumed until the issuance of the first indictment. The most that can be said about the mode of correspondence is that it was indiscreet, or at least naive, to commit even such fantasies to paper in a time when government surveillance is widespread. Neither correspondent suspected that Boyd Douglas was employing his various girl friends to copy all the letters he was transmitting in and out of Lewisburg. It is clear that the kidnaping proposal was never more than a trial balloon, but it was a balloon that led to a trial.

JANUARY TO HOLY WEEK: THE HARRISBURG TRIAL

The trial itself was going to be the political encounter of the century. However, as one reporter commented in retrospect, it was "something like being promised the apocalypse and winding up with a leaky basement."[3] Indeed, the trial itself is not as important as a number of its implications, and we will follow its course only at sufficient length to enable us to look more fully in conclusion at those implications.

The first four weeks at Harrisburg were spent on jury selection, and at the final count a jury had been chosen that can be described in many ways: one Roman Catholic, eight Protestants, three with "no religious affiliation," three who opposed the war in Vietnam, a mother of four conscientious objectors, three college graduates. Whatever other components are added or subtracted, the jury was a clear slice of "middle America," which is apparently what the government had angled for by electing to hold the trial in Harrisburg, Pennsylvania. The judge was a Nixon appointee, sixty-one years old, a member of the American Legion and the Veterans of Foreign Wars, a Moose, Lion, and Mason. The prosecuting attorney, William Lynch, was a Roman Catholic (as were his four assistants), who looked upon Pope John as a destroyer of the Catholic Church, and who stated in a pretrial motion that the government saw the defendants as "more dangerous than the mafia." The team of defense attorneys included among others Ramsey Clark, a former attorney general of the United States, and William Kunstler, who had also defended the Catonsville Nine.

The case opened formally on January 24, 1972, and ended (in one of the few religious symbols to emerge) during Holy Week, a fact to which both sides made weighty reference. The government took twenty-four days and sixty-four witnesses to present its case, although it was apparent throughout that the fourteen days given to one witness, Boyd F. Douglas, Jr., would make the government's case—or break it.

Mr. Lynch's opening statement on February 21 predictably asserted that the three parts of the first count were legitimately interrelated and that the draft board raids were warm-up exercises for the bombing and kidnaping proposals. If there had been a conspiracy around the first, it could be assumed that there had been a conspiracy around the second and third as well. The testimony of the chief witness, Boyd Douglas, Jr., would be conclusive. Ramsey Clark, in an opening statement for the defense, predictably suggested that the government was prosecuting the defendants in order to stifle the peace movement and also to "justify a leak" by J. Edgar Hoover. The testimony of the chief witness, Boyd Douglas, Jr., would be shown to be untrustworthy.

For the first week various government witnesses testified to raids on the Philadelphia draft boards, and Bucknell coeds (who first took the fifth amendment and only testified when promised full immunity) indicated that they had copied the smuggled letters for Douglas. The associate warden at Lewisburg testified that he had helped to arrange a meeting between Douglas and Father Berrigan, and a circumstantial web of evidence was gradually constructed. Certain of the government's witnesses turned out to be of no particular help to its case, particularly Ms. Jane Hoover, a friend of Douglas, who testified that he had urged her to participate in the illegal act of raiding draft boards, and that none of the defendants had ever done so. Furthermore, Douglas had told her that once he got out of prison he intended to engage in "meaningful" acts of protest, meaning "explosives" in Washington. Much of the government evidence was *pro forma*, such as the meticulous identification of the fingerprints on an explosives manual given to Father Wenderoth by Boyd Douglas, when the defense was prepared to stipulate that the fingerprints were indeed Father Wenderoth's.

Douglas finally took the stand on February 28, and was questioned and cross-examined during the fourteen days that comprised the balance of the prosecution's case. He indicated that he quickly became the confidant of Father Berrigan, and early began smuggling letters in and out of prison for him, copies of which he had made for the FBI. He described conversations, phone calls, and meetings with the other defendants (save Eqbal Ahmad whom he had never met), which he used to corroborate the material in the Berrigan-McAlister correspondence. He insisted that Father Wenderoth had told him he had fifteen people ready to participate in the tunnel bombing, and that Anthony Scoblick had assigned Douglas the task of placing explosives and teaching others how to use them. (Here was another instance in which government witnesses were curiously unhelpful to their sponsor. Witness Barone was supposed to corroborate Douglas's story about the tunnel bombing, but reported instead that the defendants had been worried from the beginning that any such project would involve unacceptable methods of violence. "[Wenderoth] made it clear," Barone testified, "that they would not go forward with anything that involved any danger to a human life.")

Under cross-examination Douglas acknowledged that from the first he was "misleading" Father Berrigan. When the defense tried to show that Douglas was not only an informer but also an *agent provocateur* (a theme to which we will return), Douglas conceded that he had told Father Berrigan that Henry Kissinger could not be kidnaped without a gun and that he could provide one. He testified that Father Berrigan had considered blowing up the computer system in the Pentagon and had reacted with "callousness" to the report of a death in a bombing at the University of Wisconsin. (Douglas's faulty chronology later showed that Berrigan could not have made such a statement to him.) He freely admitted that he had lied to the defendants many times; at the same time he insisted he would not lie in court to convict them.

The defense pressed Douglas hard under cross-examination in an attempt to break his story. He was trapped into many minor inconsistencies but no major ones. The issue at stake in his testimony was not so much whether this or that item in the account was credible; the issue was the overall credibility of the entire account. It was not the subplots of the drama that were decisive; it was the entire plot itself. Indeed, the basic issue was whether there was any plot at all beyond the one being enacted inside the head of Boyd Douglas.

Since most of what he had to say was already common knowledge, due to Mr. Hoover's initial charges and the placing of excerpts of the McAlister-Berrigan correspondence in the indictment, there was little drama in Douglas's testimony—save over the possibility that he might crack under questioning or make some egregious slip that would demolish his entire testimony. He did neither.

The greatest "drama," therefore, came when Ramsey Clark got up to begin the presentation of the case for the defense. "The defendants," Mr. Clark began, "shall always seek peace. They proclaim their innocence," he continued, "of these charges. The defense," Mr. Clark concluded, "rests." End of presentation of the case for the defense.

Now whatever might have been predicted about the unfolding of the trial, this eventuality had been foreseen by no one. Throughout the months leading up to it, the defendants had been expected to use the trial as a means of heightening political consciousness in America about the war, about governmental repression of dissent, about political prisoners, about a dozen other deeply felt concerns. So the decision not to present a defense came as a stunning surprise to the world, the press, the judge, the jury, and—probably most of all—the prosecutor, William Lynch, who had been waiting for months, as he had previously stated, for "a chance to cross-examine Liz and Phil."

As can be imagined, the decision to forego a defense had not been lightly or easily made. The "Harrisburg Seven" were split as nearly down the middle as seven persons could be; the vote was 4–3, with Father Berrigan, Sister Elizabeth and Eqbal Ahmad in the minority. Father Berrigan, in fact, bitterly disagreed with the decision and disassociated himself from his legal staff at this point in the proceedings.

A variety of reasons were given by the majority for taking the unusual and risky course they did: (1) They believed that the prosecution would use cross-examination as a "fishing expedition" to secure the names of others who had been involved in discussions about draft-board raids, and that new prosecutions would result. They wanted to keep such people free from this eventuality. (2) Since a motion for immunity for defense witnesses had been denied (although immunity had been granted to prosecution witnesses), any witnesses who testified and indicated participation in draft-board discussions or activities would also be subject to prosecution, and any who refused to testify would be subject to contempt charges. (3) The most important reason, from both a tactical and substantive point of view, was the feeling that the just-completed cross-examination of Boyd Douglas had truly destroyed his credibility, and that with this went the destruction of the case based on his testimony. It was a bold maneuver; it involved saying to the jury in effect, "You have seen how preposterous, how downright silly this whole business is. The government has disproved its case out of its own mouth. Why should we take many weeks of your time and ours to repeat the obvious? Our innocence of these charges is already plain." (4) There was probably another reason (not publicly stated as were the above three) which grew from the extraordinarily complex psychological nature of the Berrigan-McAlister correspondence, and the degree to which it could be explained to a jury in such a way as to sift out motivations, actions, fantasies, and realties in any kind of understandable way. Even taking all these factors into account, however, the risk in presenting no defense was clearly a calculated one, undertaken with no assurance that the odds were favorable.

Once the court had recovered from its surprise, the case moved into final argument by both parties. It then went to the jury, which began deliberations during Holy Week, as crowds of demonstrators appeared in Harrisburg for symbolic acts of public "liturgical" support of the defendants. Before turning the case over to the jury, however, the judge himself ruled out two of the three charges against Eqbal Ahmad, on the grounds that there was not sufficient evidence to sustain them in a court of law.

THE JURY'S DECISION—AND INDECISION

The jury was out seven days, which is a very, very, very long time for a jury to be out on a federal case. It came back to the court several times during that period for various clarifications of the meaning of "conspiracy," a blackboard, requests for portions of the transcript, etc. It indicated on each occasion that it was having considerable difficulty reaching a decision, and was admonished on each occasion by the judge to keep on trying. After thirty-three hours of deliberation, it achieved unanimous agreement on the fact that four letters from Father Berrigan had been smuggled out of prison and three letters from Sister Elizabeth had been smuggled in. This affirmation of the obvious was big news for a couple of days, since it was the only news there was. Finally, after fifty-nine hours of deliberation, it reported itself hopelessly deadlocked on the only significant charge, that of "conspiracy," and a mistrial was declared. It transpired that the jury vote had been 10–2 for acquittal of the entire group on the conspiracy charge and for acquittal of Eqbal Ahmad on the one remaining charge against him.

Thus the government's elaborate case, involving a year and a half of preparation, and the expenditure of $1,000,000–$1,500,-000, convinced only two out of twelve jurors that there was any substance to its allegations. William Lynch's rejoinder that "seven out of ten counts isn't bad," represented the epitome of a pyrrhic victory, since he lost on the only count that truly counted.[4] One of the two jurors who upheld the government gave as his reason, "If the government has spent all that money on the case there must be truth to its charges." One only hopes that this criterion for assessing the judicial competence of a governmental prosecution will not tempt future attorney generals.

A hung jury. Only two out of twelve "middle Americans" believed Boyd Douglas and the case the government built around him. Not a clear and unambiguous victory for the defense, to be sure, but by the same token a soiled and almost unambiguous defeat for the prosecution. Since the American judicial system proceeds on the assumption that defendants are innocent until proven guilty, and since they were not even close to being proven guilty, the assumption of their innocence is the continuing assumption one must make.

Once the case was over, there was a profusion of editorial comment from all over the country, with consistently widespread criticism of the government for mounting such a weak case at such great expense of time and money and human resources. Words like *shoddy* and *shabby* were frequently used. Typical of many was the comment of the St. Louis *Post-Dispatch*, even before the decision had been reached, in an editorial commenting on the "sickening spectacle" of Boyd Douglas and his testimony:

"Whatever the outcome, every decent American must be sickened by the conniving of the government's star witness, and ashamed of his government for resorting to such expedients."

MORAL IMPLICATIONS OF THE TRIAL

As was stated earlier, the trial itself is not as important as some of the overall issues it raises, and it is to the moral implications of the trial that we now turn. Four concerns will be discussed.

1. *The government's use of the conspiracy charge.* To a layman, the charge of "conspiracy" sounds sinister and subversive. This is partly due to the government's lavish use of the charge in recent political trials, since to "con-spire" means literally only "to breathe together," which can be done for good ends as well as for ill. The beauty of a conspiracy charge, from the government's point of view, is that not very much needs to be proved. It need not be shown that the defendants *did* the things they talked about, or even that they all talked about them together (Eqbal Ahmad and Philip Berrigan, for example, had never met one another until after the indictment had been issued linking them in a conspiracy). All that need be shown is that there was some kind of agreement to commit an unlawful act and that at least one "overt act" was committed in the process of moving toward that end. In both indictments, phone calls and letters were the chief examples of "overt acts."

In the use of the conspiracy charge in the present case, however, a clever, if diabolical, move was made by the government, to which attention has already been called. This was to shift the substantive character of the charge between Mr. Hoover's first announcement, the initial indictment, and the second indictment. As we have seen, all the publicity centered on the conspiracy to bomb buildings and kidnap Kissinger. It was not until the second indictment, however, that the charge of conspiring to raid draft boards was introduced, but since the three kinds of activity were linked in a single count of the indictment, this meant (as the

judge patiently reminded the jury on a number of occasions)
that evidence of guilt on *any one* of the three was sufficient to
prove conspiracy. So the scenario that emerged went like this:
first, make extravagant charges, then, late in the game couple
them with a relatively modest charge, secure conviction on the
modest charge and leave the impression that conviction has
thereby been procured on the extravagant charges.

But beyond the fact that the conspiracy charge was so cynically
and frighteningly abused by the government in this particular
instance, there is an even greater moral danger in its widespread
use, even if one could assume good faith on the part of the prosecution—an assumption that is increasingly difficult to make.
The danger is that the use of the conspiracy charge in political
trials of this sort becomes an enormously potent weapon for
stifling free assembly and the free expression of opinion, even if
convictions are not ultimately secured. When one believes that
his government is engaging in a patently monstrous evil (an
opinion that in this case each of the defendants conscientiously
held about the Vietnam war), then it is incumbent upon him to
say so, not only for the sake of his own conscience but for the
moral health of his country. Individuals and groups must then be
free to explore all possible ways in which the evil can be stopped.
From a moral perspective, there must be *no restraint whatever*
on what is thinkable and speakable. All ideas deserve to be expressed and reacted to, both for the positive purpose of creating
and refining new modes of expression and action, and also for the
negative purpose of being beaten down and discarded as silly,
impractical, or immoral.

Thus it is useful and important that a group of pacifists, for
example, committed to nonviolence, re-examine the nature of that
commitment from time to time, to see whether, in the light of new
facts and circumstances, the commitment is still valid. Such
people *must* be free to say to one another, "Maybe things have
gotten so bad that we must rethink our position. Maybe nonviolence is now a moral cop out, since the establishment can
absorb it without having to change its policies. Maybe we ought

to move to a citizen's arrest of somebody, or disrupt the working of some government buildings, or something like that." And then, having been expressed, the idea can be batted around. In the case of the Harrisburg Seven it is clear that the idea was batted around, not very seriously, and then batted down and discarded as kooky, impractical, and involving an unacceptable degree of potential violence that could destroy human lives.

What is so disturbing about the Harrisburg trial is that it was precisely *this* sort of informal, unstructured, and quickly discarded weekend chatter that the government tried to transform into a sinister plot that made the defendants "more dangerous to America than organized crime." This means that anyone the government wants to silence it can silence—or (in the light of the jury's response) can try to silence, for who has not made casual remarks that could be interpreted in another context in sinister fashion, and who wants to go through the pain and expense and potential destructiveness of a long political trial for the sake of casual remarks? To know that casual talk and very casual letter writing can have such severe consequences is surely to have received explicit instructions from one's government that unless one wants his own life seriously interrupted if not destroyed, he had better not voice even the mildest sort of protest.

Which, it would appear, must ultimately have been the government's purpose in raising the issue at all. For even without a strong case, the threats that the weak case poses—that the net of suspicion and intimidation will spread yet wider—makes the gamble on the government's part worth taking. It is better to have bluffed and lost than never to have bluffed at all.

2. *The government's use of informers and agents provocateurs.* In order to get evidence of conspiracy by private citizens, the government must gain access to their thoughts and words, and these are not, after all, usually shouted from the housetops. It is here that a second important moral implication of the Harrisburg trial emerges; for the government gets such evidence by using paid spies, stool pigeons, informers, and *agents provocateurs.*

What are we to say about the role of the Boyd Douglases in this and similar cases?[5]

The life of the *agent provocateur* may be very complex, but the concept is very simple. He is a paid employee of the government who by a variety of deceptions and lies insinuates his way into the confidence and workings of a group of which the government feels it has reason to be suspicious. His role is not only to spy and inform upon and thereby betray his newly won "friends"; for such purposes the term *agent* alone would suffice. His role is also to "provoke," i.e. to call forth or suggest, certain ideas and courses of action that will make it possible for the government to secure an airtight indictment. When necessary, the *agent provocateur* will go beyond mere suggestion; he will procure vital information in illegal ways, secure explosives, get guns, and take leadership in the action that his own suggestions and involvement have led the group to undertake.

Much of the cross-examination of Boyd Douglas was devoted to trying to show that he was not only an informer or agent, which nobody doubted, but that he was also an *agent provocateur*. Cumulative evidence emerges from the testimony that it was he who made repeated attempts to provoke the group to levels of violence that were his own idea and not theirs; it was he, not those indicted, who tried to persuade Bucknell coeds to engage in illegal antiwar activities; it was he who insisted that a gun would be needed to kidnap Kissinger and stated that he could provide one; it was he who wrote a political science professor at Bucknell suggesting the destruction of the ROTC building; it was he who (in an extraordinarily "provocative" act) gave two manuals on explosives to Father Wenderoth, manuals that another FBI agent had procured for him from the aforementioned ROTC building at Bucknell. In these and other instances there was an attempt to "provoke" people to levels of activity and violence that were not their own idea but his. It is further important to note that even if the attempt does not succeed, the *provocateur* has moved the level of discussion into new areas, and hypothetical possibilities, even when discarded, will have been discussed in ways that can be exceedingly damaging when reported to the public later on solely through the interpretive words of the *provocateur*.

We can see the implications of the role of the *agent provocateur* even more clearly by looking at a parallel example. During the Harrisburg trial, another *agent provocateur*, Robert Hardy, released an account of his own involvement in the raids on the Camden, New Jersey, draft boards. Mr. Hardy, a parishioner of one of the priests involved in plans to raid the Camden draft board, had initially gone to the FBI because of his concern "to stop the action." The FBI told him to watch developments and later *ordered him to make the raid happen.* Hardy stated in his affidavit that the defendants in the case seemed to have discarded the idea until he rekindled their interest, and that without his leadership and FBI financing, the Camden draft board raid could never have taken place. It was Hardy, then, who trained them for the raid, got floor plans of the offices, maps of the area, and also provided the finances, which in turn were provided by the FBI. He even urged the participants to escalate their plans to include violence—one bit of advice they refused to follow. In sum, Hardy stated in his affidavit, the raid "definitely wouldn't have happened without me."[6]

The issue then is broader than Boyd Douglas, who is only one illustration of the problem. It might be arguable on some level of practical realism about the baleful nature of the human situation, that in a fallen world governments must have agents who seek to discover ahead of time what "the enemy" is planning, so as to forestall such actions by the development of effective counter-measures. Even if this were granted, a number of basic moral questions about the use of *agents provocateurs* can be raised:

(a) More careful discrimination is needed in determining who really *is* "the enemy" who must be apprehended. The notion that Mr. Hoover and the nation were seriously imperiled by a handful of priests and nuns known to be resolutely committed to non-violence and engaging in a variety of protest actions against an immoral war, and that these people were really (as Mr. Lynch insisted) a greater threat to American security than "the mafia," shows a disconcerting lack of discrimination about priorities. Indeed, the counterargument can be advanced that the moral health of the nation is not only improved but even dependent upon the witness of dissent that the Father Phils and the Sister Lizes have provided over the past decade. The present widespread American disenchantment with the war has not come about because of the J. Edgar Hoovers or the Richard Nixons or the MacGeorge Bundys, but because of the moral stance of what was initially a tiny handful of war protesters, who deserve our national gratitude rather than our federal indictments.

(b) The use of the *agent provocateur* also raises the question of the degree to which good ends, such as integrity in national life and government, can be served by evil means, such as deception, lies, provocation action and overall deceit. When a government must base what it considers a moral case on the unsavory testimony and actions of a Boyd Douglas as its chief and only significant witness, we are witnessing in our turn the moral decay of government to a shabby and demeaned level, from which none of the high moral protestations of White House spokesmen effectively can rescue it. Francine du Plessix Gray does not mince words in commenting on this:

The F.B.I.'s indifference, its lack of control over Douglas's acts, is appalling, even if it had not been aware that he was also a provocateur. This use of a man with a pathological record of lying and violence, let loose upon a sheltered campus, offering guns, explosive manuals, and advice for the destruction of buildings to students, teachers and visiting priests, seems to me one of the shoddiest chapters to date in the annals of government infiltration.[7]

(c) Even if one could make the case for the professional *agent provocateur*, the decision of the government to enlist the services of private citizens in that capacity is morally alarming. Boyd Douglas already had a long list of convictions for lying, stealing, forging, and deceiving, and was being punished by society for engaging in such misdeeds. By accepting him as an informer and *provocateur*, the government suddenly began to reward him for practicing precisely those deficiencies of character for which it had previously been punishing him. In using private citizens in this way the government reverses every canon of morality upon which a democratic society should be based, transforms vice into virtue, and pays handsome rewards to those who will engage in betrayal. It is no wonder that a Boyd Douglas, tasting such newly found moral approbation and financial largesse, should continually seek to up the financial ante of what his revelations were worth.

(d) This leads to a related point. When a person already willing to deceive and bear false witness is handsomely reimbursed by his government for so doing, the temptation is almost irresistible to increase the scope of the evidence he communicates. If he started out only as an informer, he will be tempted to "provoke" more extreme attitudes and actions so that he will have more to report, and so that his own usefulness to the government, and consequently his own rewards, will be greater. He faces an almost irresistible urge to reveal more than there actually is to reveal. One would hope that before they employ more Boyd Douglases, the future counterparts of J. Edgar Hoover and John Mitchell will read Graham Green's *Our Man in Havana* for an illustration of how a private citizen, enlisted as an agent by his government, creates an entire conspiracy out of whole cloth in order to satisfy his ego and keep those satisfying checks coming from headquarters.

(e) This placing of a premium on dishonesty, duplicity, and double-dealing leads one to ask how far the statements of an *agent provocateur* should be believed and trusted, even under oath in court. That the individual is extraordinarily adept at lying is one of the chief tools of his trade; why, then, should his word suddenly become trustworthy simply because it is now to the advantage of the government to believe him? (One notes with dismay the government's attempt to build up the character of Boyd Douglas who had favorable testimony to offer, and almost simultaneously attempt to destroy the character of Dita Beard, in the ITT case, who had unfavorable testimony to offer.) A government case built almost exclusively on the testimony of a man hired by that government to deceive, is likely to be a deception itself. The need of the government to overcome this obvious moral handicap is nowhere better illustrated than by the fact that the prosecutor, William Lynch, could *seriously* claim in court that Douglas now had a "sterling character." Either Lynch believed this, in which case his own moral values are called into serious question, or he did not believe this, in which case his own moral values are called into serious question.

(f) There is a moral question about the violation of human integrity that is involved in the case of the *provocateur*. Even if two people are in genuine and not spurious agreement about a desired end, such as ending the war, they may have legitimate differences about the most appropriate ways of attaining that end. And it becomes a serious violation of personhood if either partner tries to coerce the other into a kind of action for which he or she is not yet morally or psychically ready.

The situation of the *agent provocateur*, however, is at a double remove from this situation, for he not only does not share genuinely the ultimate aims of the group into which he has insinuated himself, but he is also dedicated to forcing its members into positions they might themselves not arrive at, and to do things that without him they might never have done. His role, in other words, is purely manipulative; if those he is seeking to incriminate do not themselves initiate incriminating actions, he will find ways to see that they do. He sees them not as persons to whom to relate, but as objects to be manipulated to his own (and the government's) ends.

(g) The widespread use of *agents provocateur* further extends the problem we examined in the case of the conspiracy charge, namely the "chilling effect" a government produces that militates against open and honest discussion that is critical of the government. As any group grows beyond a few initial members, all of whom know one another well, there is increasing need to guard one's statements and to cultivate a suspicious rather than a trusting attitude toward new members, for fear one of them may be a government informer or *provocateur*. Freedom of expression becomes significantly curtailed and the very lifeblood of a democracy is imperiled. The practice is wide enough in dictatorial regimes to make those committed to the democratic process exceedingly critical of a government that uses the informer and *provocateur* as stock-in-trade devices to inhibit discussion and protest. By the very nature of the need for secrecy, we know little about the full use of *agents provocateur* by the FBI and the justice department. The more one probes, however, the more one feels that only the tip of the iceberg has become visible. We used to be able to assume that in a democratic society police were on hand to prevent crimes rather than to encourage or commit them. No more.

3. *The Church's role as a community of dissent.* Thus far we have looked at implications of the Harrisburg trial raised by the involvement of the government. We must now look at the implications raised by the involvement of the defendants. Much of the government's appeal to the jury and to the American people was based on the supposed impropriety of priests and nuns "getting involved" in political activity of any sort. It is their job, so the argument ran, "to deal with the things of the spirit." Thus we have raised for us the whole question of the Church as a community of dissent within the wider community of the state.

(a) The Church may be more than simply the community of dissent but it can never be less, and our initial comment must be that "the case for dissent" and even for civil disobedience, is crystal clear in Christian history. The Judaic roots out of which Christianity sprang were nurtured by the First Commandment, "You shall have no other gods before me," "gods" being the term used to designate one's ultimate allegiance, which, in the case of Israel, could mean loyalty to the god of another nation or even loyalty to one's own nation in such a way that it usurps the place

of the true God and seeks to take his place by demanding the kind
of allegiance that belongs to him alone. The latter dimension has
always been constitutive of the Christian posture of dissent, for it
is always the temptation of the nation to demand the kind of
unqualified allegiance ("My country right or wrong . . .") that
belongs to God alone. The same point is made by Peter, who
responds to a demand by the court with the words, "We must
obey God rather than men." It is embedded in the earliest Christian confession, *Kurios Christos,* "Christ is Lord," a political as
well as a theological confession, since it directly challenged the
then-regnant confession of citizens of the Roman Empire, *Kurios
Caesar,* "Caesar [the State] is Lord." Saint Thomas More, com-
manded by his sovereign to engage in a course of action he felt
was wrong, and challenged as to whether he was or was not "the
King's good servant," replied, "I am, Sire, the King's good servant, but I am God's good servant first."

All of this (and much more) is central to the Christian understanding of how one acts responsibly toward the state. One *is*
responsible to the state, but if the demands of the state and the
demands of God conflict, it is acting responsibly toward the state
to dissent from its demands, since a state that flouts God's will is
a state on the way to its own destruction. The dissenter must
appeal from the state ill-informed to the state better informed,
and do so in the light of his own Christian vision.

When the state needs to be corrected, those who wish to bring
about change start out by "working within the system," and the
Berrigans and their friends were no exception. But, as we saw in
the early pages of this essay, the twin escalations of the horror of
the war abroad, and the government's repression at home of those
who dissented from the horror, forced those with sensitive con-
sciences like the Harrisburg Seven to move further and further
along the spectrum of active dissent and finally into civil disobedience.

Their course was further dictated by the unwillingness of their
church to become involved, until very late in the day, in any kind
of moral condemnation of the war. There are sins of commission,

and there are sins of omission, and the "sin of silence" of American bishops and other church leaders gave antiwar churchmen no other option than to move into more vigorous statement and action in an attempt to communicate their morally crucial message. As Francine Gray ironically remarks, "I held the Catholic hierarchy as ultimately responsible for the Berrigans' so-called radicalism." In the final weighing of the balances, as to where the "responsible" Christian voices were located in America in relation to Vietnam, it is increasingly clear that the responsible voices will turn out to have been those of conscientious objectors, the draft resisters, the protesters who went to jail rather than remain silent, the Catonsville Nine, the Baltimore Eight, the Harrisburg Seven. These people were not distortions of the Christian conscience but exemplars of it in the face of powerful evil. Jail is not an unusual place for a Christian of sensitive conscience to be, as any reading of the New Testament will make clear.

(b) Allied to the issue of dissent, which is clear-cut, is the issue of the use of violence in the exercise of that dissent, which is far from clear-cut. It was the argument of the prosecution that the defendants had moved, or were preparing to move, from non-violent to violent acts of protest. It was the ongoing contention of the defendants that their commitment to nonviolence remained consistent.

The issue is difficult to open up, particularly in brief compass, since the word *violence* is subject to such a wide variety of interpretations and definitions. Surely one of the major considerations of the Berrigans and the nonviolent "Catholic left" has been their belief that personhood must not be violated and that no actions can be allowed that bring physical harm to anyone. As Daniel Berrigan said while he was underground in a taped message to the Weathermen, the violence-prone wing of the student left, "There is no principle that is worth the sacrifice of a single human life." This is a hard saying, which Daniel Berrigan recognized, but it is consistent with the viewpoint he expressed after reading

Eberhard Bethge's biography of Dietrich Bonhoeffer, that he could not go along with Bonhoeffer in the decision to take part in the plot against Hitler's life. It is consistent also with the fact that on a number of occasions the defendants at Harrisburg had drawn back from specific proposals for war protest on the grounds that they might endanger human lives.

But there is a further factor in any consideration of violence, and it was delineated by the defendants at the time of their initial arraignment: Who are the real purveyors of violence in our society? It can be argued that they are those in our society who create and maintain situations of injustice by which in subtle but devastating ways personhood is violated, even though no overt physical acts are involved. The "violence of the slum," not simply the violence *in* the slum, but the violence *of* the slum, would be a case in point. The situation is even more clear-cut, of course, when overt physical acts of violence are employed in order to maintain an existing situation of injustice. This, the defendants have argued for years, was the situation with American military power in Vietnam, which represented, so they felt, a use of overt violence so naked and ugly that strong measures were called for in order to try to counteract it. And so the defendants asked a question at their arraignment that must leave all Americans uncomfortable: "We ask our fellow citizens to match our lives, our actions, against the actions of the president, his advisers, his chiefs of staff, and we pose the question: who has committed the crimes of violence?"

"Who has committed the crimes of violence?" One is hard put to defend the notion that Philip Berrigan is guilty of violence while Richard Nixon is not, or that Sister Elizabeth should be in jail while Secretaries of Defense go free.

The question is not going to disappear when the Harrisburg trial is forgotten, or Vietnam is no longer the scene of bloodshed. For "crimes of violence" will continue to be a prime moral problem in the crucial decades ahead. The experience of certain "Christian revolutionaries" in the third world is instructive on this point. Camile Torres, the Colombian priest who finally joined the guerilla forces and was shot, believed that the decision about whether social change would come violently or nonviolently would be made not by the guerilla forces but by the minority holding power; either the few with inordinate power would relinquish some of it voluntarily, in which case change would come nonviolently, or the inordinate power would have to be taken from them, in which case overt violence would be the only means left of achieving change. His assumption was that covert violence, in the form of widespread injustice, *already existed* in a society run by a very few for their own benefit, to the dehumanization of the great majority of those who were powerless victims of that injustice.

If the violence of injustice continues, and if powerful governments not only tolerate it but actually perpetuate it and are unwilling to listen to cries of moral outrage, then sooner or later at least some of those who up to now have engaged in nonviolent protest will feel morally bound to cross the line to violence, as the only pressure those with power can understand. And who, if that day comes, will have been guilty of the ongoing "crimes of violence," the perpetuation of injustices that finally necessitated a new politics of moral desperation when all lesser vehicles had proven inefficacious?

(c) A further problem raised by the posture of dissent has to do with the assessment the dissenters make of human nature. Can those whose thoughts and motivations may have a relatively high degree of moral "purity" really measure the fallenness that may characterize the thoughts and motivations of another? Put less grandiosely, do those engaging in selfless social protest react naively to the evil that may be present in those with whom they are involved? Put bluntly, how could the defendants have been taken in so completely by Boyd Douglas?

Francine Gray, who knows several of the defendants personally, has a helpful answer to this question. She sees their trust "as a phenomenon of the 1960s, rising from that sympathy for the dispossessed that has marked the conscience of American liberals since the nascence of the civil rights movement." Most of those

associated with Douglas acknowledge that they had to overcome
an initial distrust by sheer acts of will, feeling that it was "elitist"
or "bourgeois" to doubt the victims of the system. I believe we
can construct a syllogism to express this trust:

> Society distrusts Boyd Douglas.
> But society's values are themselves to be distrusted.
> Therefore Boyd Douglas can be trusted.

Mrs. Gray is critical: "[Philip] Berrigan's faith in Douglas suggests that absolute Christianity may be irreconcilable with traditional political action and with the precautionary measures essential to effective political behavior."[8]

She may be right, and the defendants might even agree with
her terms, acknowledging that they no longer have any interest in
"traditional political action" or "effective political behavior,"
and that a witness must be made regardless of its political consequences. They might further argue that a Christian, and particularly a priest or a nun, is called upon to have unqualified trust
even in the untrustworthy, that such an act is a paradigm of
divine grace, and that the Christian must be willing to suffer on
behalf of ongoing trust in the ongoing betrayer.

One could not fault the right of an individual to make such a
decision and to suffer such consequences himself, but the matter
becomes more complicated when the betrayer brings down not
only the one who trusted, but others who invested similar trust
and were likewise betrayed. This is only a way of saying, at slight
remove, that such an uncalculating trust in Boyd Douglas led to
the Berrigan-McAlister correspondence, which led in turn to the
indictment of all the others and to the capture of Daniel Berrigan.

Even granting that, we have no right to be too harsh on the
individuals involved, since all of them, and Father Wenderoth in
particular, continued *even after Douglas's betrayal of them was
complete* to manifest an ongoing concern for him as a person, and
to believe that it was not yet too late for his moral rehabilitation.
A priestly concern remained, even after the priests themselves
had been betrayed. Indeed, one of the defense lawyers later con-

fessed that he was both personally impressed and professionally hamstrung in his months of preparing the defense that was never used by the unwillingness of any of the defendants to seek to ensure their freedom at the cost of "destroying" Douglas.

So the issue of the Christian apprehension of the forces of evil at work in ambiguous situations itself remains ambiguous after the trial. Doubtless the defendants would argue that it can never be wrong to have faith in another human being; doubtless, too, they would be exceedingly careful another time in choosing couriers for extralegal correspondence.

4. *The remaining enigma: Why was the case ever prosecuted?* A final issue may be raised about the implications of the trial as a whole. It is posed by Betty Medsger in an article written at the conclusion of the trial: "And so the Government's case fell of its own weight, leaving still other questions unanswered: Why was this case prosecuted? And why was the Justice Department willing to endure the inevitable embarrassment of such flimsy evidence?"[9] The question is a fascinating one—fascinating not only in the sense of being interesting and intriguing, but also in the sense of drawing one to the very borders of the uncanny and forbidding and even frightening. Here was a palpably weak case based on the most dubious kind of evidence—a case so unconvincing that it was convincingly rebutted merely by a decision not to engage in a rebuttal. Why, then, the $1,000,000 to $1,500,000 spent, the amassing of such a high-power legal team, the extraordinary publicity, all for a lost cause? Probably no one knows the full answer, but there would seem to be at least two interconnected reasons:

(a) The Justice Department had been presented with a *fait accompli* in the form of Mr. Hoover's original unsubstantiated charges against Daniel and Philip Berrigan. Somewhere a decision had to be made either to leave Mr. Hoover publicly and permanently embarrassed, or to get him off the hook. Somewhere the latter decision was obviously made. An indictment was hastily drawn up—so hastily and poorly that it had to be replaced with a second and different one—and a trial was held. It was a costly way to save face—the face of one man—not only in terms of taxpayers' money but also in terms of damage to human lives and the expending of much of whatever remaining credibility the administration might still have possessed.

The theme of saving face applies not only to Mr. Hoover, but also to the ongoing embarrassment that the nonviolent wing of the "peace movement" had become to the FBI and the Justice Department. The latter had been notoriously unsuccessful in preventing draft board raids by the "East Coast Conspiracy to Save Lives," or in securing convictions after the raids had been carried out, while the former had incurred four months of the humiliation of having Daniel Berrigan "underground" but surfacing frequently in the sight of almost everybody but the FBI agents who were supposed to have the expertise to capture him. There was lots of egg on lots of faces.

What eventuated in the Harrisburg trial thus became a chance to even up some old scores. If the nonviolent wing of war protest was an increasing embarrassment to the administration, a maneuver that would both discredit the nonviolent wing of war protest and restore credibility to law-enforcement agencies was surely tempting. To imply, and then "prove," that the leadership of nonviolent war protest had moved from nonviolence to violence—betraying both its principles and its followers—appears to have been a road too inviting not to walk down.

(b) An even more important reason why the government must have persisted with the case can only be described as another example—perhaps the crowning one—of a moral flaw in the attitude of the Nixon administration. This flaw is the persistent attempt to use the judicial process to destroy dissent. The attorney general, the Justice Department, the FBI and the White House seem united in this concern; from the very beginning there were promises from all quarters "to crack down on dissenters." The attitude is evidenced in the political trials of the last four years; in the stepped-up prosecution of draft resisters; in the

attempts to use the courts against political threats: from the
Chicago Seven to the New York Black Panthers to Huey Newton
to Angela Davis to the Harrisburg Seven to Daniel Ellsberg,
along with many other trials less widely publicized. It is evidenced
in the initiation of "no-knock legislation" from Mr. Mitchell's
office and by the futile zeal with which both he and Mr. Nixon
pushed for two consecutive Supreme Court appointments the
Senate was unprecedentedly unwilling to confirm. It is evidenced
by the sneering contempt former Vice President Agnew reserved
for dissenters, and by the extravagance of Mr. Lynch's asserting
in all seriousness that the defendants at Harrisburg were more
dangerous to the United States than the leaders of organized
crime. It is evidenced, most recently, in Mr. Haldeman's uncontrolled glee that a demonstration against the president and Billy
Graham might become violent and thus be able to be manipulated
by the White House to discredit war protest.

One might call the defendants an embarrassment to an administration waging an unjust war; one might call them im-
prudent or downright silly; one might call them exemplars of
moral courage and feel judged thereby; but to call them criminals, to prosecute them and to attempt to place them in prison, is
such a defensive reaction against challenge, and substantively so
far-fetched and implausible as to call into serious question either
the good judgment or the good faith—or both—of the political
machine that insisted on so doing.

Few things more need challenging in a democracy than the
syndrome of trying to destroy dissent judicially. As we reflect on
the jury's verdict at Harrisburg, we can only be glad that the
people are still wiser than their government.

NOTES

1. An excellent resource for the events leading up to the trial is the
Holy Cross Quarterly, vol. 4, no. 1, January 1971, esp. pp. 70–76, "Hoover
and the Berrigans."

2. "Harrisburg: The Politics of Salvation," *New York Review of Books*,

June 15, 1972, p. 16. This series of two articles, which appeared in the June 1, 1972 (pp. 34–40) and June 15 (pp. 14–22) issues, is the most perceptive treatment to date of the trial and the events leading up to it. For further background on the Berrigans and other figures of the Catholic left, see also her *Divine Disobedience* (New York: Knopf, 1970).

3. Sheldon Smith, *National Review*, April 28, 1972, p. 456.

4. The seven counts of smuggling letters could have brought convictions of up to forty years, but such sentencing did not transpire. De facto the practice goes on all the time in prisons and is acknowledged without ever being prosecuted.

5. In preparing this section I have been greatly aided by an as yet unpublished manuscript by Craig Schindler, a graduate of the Stanford University Law School, appropriately entitled "An Investigation of the Use of *Agents Provocateur* by Political Police in the United States, or Support Your Local Radicals—They May Be Police." This is a fully documented and chilling account of dozens of cases in which undercover FBI agents have actually been the *provocateurs* of bombings, shootings, draft board raids, etc.

6. *Los Angeles Times*, March 16, 1972, p. 8.

7. Gray, op. cit., June 1, 1972, p. 39.

8. Gray, op. cit., June 15, 1972, p. 14.

9. Medsger, "Conspiracy: On Trial at Harrisburg," *Christianity and Crisis*, May 15, 1972, p. 1211.

In the final weighing of the balances, as to where the "responsible" Christian voices were located in America in relation to Vietnam, it is increasingly clear that the responsible voices will turn out to have been those of the conscientious objectors, the draft resisters, the protesters, who went to jail rather than remain silent.

—Robert McAfee Brown

The harshest way to put what I am saying is that Daniel and Philip have become Uncle Toms. Their words about their own people—Catholic, immigrant, Irish—are characteristically harsh. . . . They concentrate on the sons and daughters of the educated classes, the college goers: resisters, Weathermen, movement people. . . . I find their course—if not wrong in itself—then politically misguided and morally romantic. . . . Yet, for many, on a cold night, it offered beauty enough to warm their hands at.

—Michael Novak

"Blue-Bleak Embers ... Fall, Gall Themselves ... Gash Gold-Vermilion" *

MICHAEL NOVAK

But if someone sets out to fight his battles in the world in his own absolute freedom, if he values the necessary deed more highly than the spotlessness of his own conscience and reputation, if he is prepared to sacrifice a fruitless principle to a fruitful compromise, or for that matter the fruitless wisdom of the *via media* to a fruitful radicalism, then let him beware lest precisely his supposed freedom may ultimately prove his undoing. He will easily consent to the bad, knowing full well that it is bad, in order to ward off what is worse, and in doing this he will no longer be able to see that precisely the worse which he is trying to avoid may still be the better. This is one of the underlying themes of tragedy.

—Dietrich Bonhoeffer, *Letters and Papers from Prison*

WHAT BONHOEFFR DOESN'T TELL US, in this quotation, is how to avoid tragedy—or whether there is any way at all. All of us are implicated in pervasive evils; all are under judgment.

For some years I have wanted to write in criticism of the moral and political positions publicly taken by Daniel and Philip Berri-

---

* The title line is from Gerard Manley Hopkins' poem "The Windhover," in which God redeems all things, especially those that fail. A comparison between the "dark night" of Daniel Berrigan and the "terrible years" in the life of Hopkins, also a Jesuit, begs to be accomplished.

MICHAEL NOVAK has written extensively on the Catholic Church, the war in Vietnam, and the plight of ethnic Americans. Among his recent books are *The Experience of Nothingness* and *Belief and Unbelief*. Mr. Novak was a speech writer for Sargent Shriver during the 1972 election and is presently planning a new program in the humanities for the Rockefeller Foundation.

gan. So long as they were attacked from all sides, especially by the government, and so long as both were in prison, unable to respond, it seemed unfair to speak. There were plenty of other moral and political positions in far greater need of criticism. I kept my peace. Now both Dan and Phil are free. The times have cooled. Perhaps it is useful to argue issues of conscience in a forum open to public criticism; and to reflect on elements in the Catholic tradition that led to Catonsville and Harrisburg—and beyond.

I have no desire to write from a position of judgment or of noninvolvement. There is reason to believe that at least one of the Catonsville Nine, David Darst, was influenced by articles of mine in *Commonweal* on themes of radical politics. After the auto accident in which he was killed, copies of an article of mine strewed the highway—he had intended to use them at a lecture he was on his way to give. In 1967, I took part in a week-long antiwar blockade of the Selective Service office in Oakland, and was luckily not among those arrested. Gradually, I came to disagree with the class basis and the biases of "the movement."

Half my soul, then, is attracted to what the Berrigans did; half of me wishes I had been with them. Their pull upon something special in the Catholic conscience was great. Many of my Catholic friends—Robert Hoyt, Peter Steinfels, Garry Wills—found it necessary, later, to "get arrested" as the Berrigans had. Just as I more and more hated (because it was hard to resist) the whole idea.

Before Catonsville and afterwards, I had fantasized actions of resistance. I rejected those fantasies. Perhaps this essay is an attempt to say why I did not follow the Berrigans, why I found their course—if not wrong in itself—then politically misguided and morally romantic. Why I resist *that* half of my soul as "a temptation."

In the end, I suppose, I believe that the Berrigans were acting out of personal (specifically priestly) needs of the Berrigans— that they wrested a certain moral, public, and political beauty from these needs—that they had insufficiently escaped a peculiarly Catholic moralism, romanticism, and clericalism.

In *No Bars to Manhood,* Daniel Berrigan alludes to the common background he shared with Francis Cardinal Spellman, a background that led the two of them to inevitable conflict—and to analogous routes of escape. The parents of Phil and Dan, *mutatis mutandis,* could have been the parents of Francis; their childhood neighborhoods and the thin alphabet soup of hard times could have been interchanged. They have each, after suffering, been endeared to opposite establishments.

There lies in nearly every Catholic of immigrant stock a terrible ambivalence. This ambivalence has two faces, an ambivalence regarding America on the one hand and liberalism on the other.

Pro deo et pro patria. Over how many portals to parochial schools are these words inscribed! As if to say: "You are not regarded as American, my children. They say you will dig tunnels from the Vatican to the White House. You will destroy the tissues of American liberty. You are authoritarian. You breed too much. Your politicians are corrupt. There are criminal tendencies in abundance in your midst. You lack the social graces. You have not read enough. You lack intellectual traditions. You practice censorship. Your ways are not American." And so, Catholic children with innocent voices pledged allegiance to the flag of the United States of America, and set out to prove that they were not pigs, but men. Becoming men—no bars to manhood—became one of the great motifs of all their lives. In 1914–18, when Poles numbered 4 percent of the population, they accepted 11 percent of the casualties.

But many immigrants retained their suspicions of self-complacent America, and its "establishment," and its "liberal" traditions. The Berrigans are not unconventional when they faintly curl their lips around the word "liberal," and speak with disdain of a powerful "establishment." Many immigrant priests have done the same.

For over a generation, with official collusion, the Ku Klux Klan terrorized Catholics as well as Blacks. No civilized nation had so bloody and violent a labor union history—and labor was, in good measure, immigrant labor. Congress passed blatantly anti-Catholic (and anti-Oriental) immigration laws. Anti-Catholicism ran deep as an almost unchecked bigotry among liberals and intellectuals. Catholics at Harvard, Yale, and Stanford were under implicit quotas more stringent than those for Jews. The "public" schools served as agents of explicit Protestant culture and of forced "Americanization." One out of every four immigrants— despite poverty, hardship, family responsibilities, and the blockades of World War I—returned to Europe. Despite official blandishments, this country treated its immigrants more cruelly and brutally than their descendants today care to recall. "We were dung," Louis Adamic wrote in recollection.

In America but not *of* it. Neither Europeans any longer, nor yet quite Americans. And not at all trusting of the great establishments: the universities, the banks, the corporations, the State Department, the federal bureaucracy, the press, the cinema. A ghetto mentality. A siege mentality. A hefty sense of the evil of the modern world. A learned distrust of social engineers, pragmatists, experts in white coats. The day Cardinal Cushing of Boston first agreed to accept an invitation to be present at a Harvard commencement, after generations of antagonism between archdiocese and university, was hardly a decade ago.

When Daniel and Philip Berrigan reject the pale pieties of liberals, they do not do so as jaundiced Brahmins whose liberal pedigree is generations old. When they assault the modern American State, it is not as if their forebears had long held high hopes for it. When they speak and act as men under siege, men who must resist, men who must say *no,* they speak in a long line of American priests who did not believe the public relations of America, who stood outside the American consensus.

The chapter in American Catholic history celebrating the victory of liberals was very brief—barely a decade long. If we date it from 1958, the year in which the Fund for the Republic set up a meeting of intellectuals to discuss Catholicism in America, thus making Catholics (even some real live ones who were present) *worthy* of discussion; and then go forward until disillusionment began setting in—the beginning of the "radical" draft raids in 1967—we encapsulate the high water marks: the inauguration of John F. Kennedy in January, 1960, and the halcyon days of the Second Vatican Council convened by Pope John from 1962 to 1965. For a brief period magazines, newspapers, and television shows couldn't get enough stories about the "new" liberal Catholicism. Daniel Berrigan himself recalls what it was like to be alive in those days, full of hope and on the flood tide of normality. But it wasn't normality. It was an interlude between two sieges.

No wonder the Berrigans are celebrated even by a political and theological conservative like Garry Wills. Wills has always been antiliberal. The highwater mark of Catholic liberalism was hard on him; he was often, as in the pages of the *National Catholic Reporter*, the token conservative. He belonged rather to the cozy world of Bill Buckley's *National Review* than to the cozy world of John Cogley's *Commonweal*. (All small magazines create—to their detractors—cozy worlds.) Becoming disillusioned with what passes, in America, for conservatism, he pictured liberalism as a way of life epitomized in Richard Nixon, whom he called "the last liberal"—a view calculated to astound those who might have thought of John Dewey, or Adlai Stevenson, or John Kenneth Galbraith as liberals. But in a day when it is as fashionable to skewer liberals from the left as it once was from the right, Wills' own antiliberal presuppositions go unnoticed and unexamined. His Chestertonian romanticism and extravagance suit a time of disarray; ruins excite the Catholic romantic splendidly. After 1968, as before 1958, a liberal Catholic is hard to find.

That the actions of the Berrigans are specifically Catholic has been widely noted. Few Protestant ministers or radical intellectuals, even among those who praise them, take them as models for action. Robert McAfee Brown describes them as "signs" rather than as "models"—stimulants of conscience, but not quite patterns for behavior.

I have heard two interpretations offered for what is explicitly Catholic in the Berrigans. First, it is said, Catholics have a powerful liturgical sense; they create liturgies almost spontaneously: burning papers at Catonsville, spilling blood on open files. An incarnational, sacramental tradition. As Eugene McCarthy said of New Hampshire in 1968: "A cause needs a person to personify it." The tradition of witness. Of deeds. Of martyrs. Catholics as dramatic, Protestants as verbal and rational. Protestants as moralistic; Catholics as sacramental.

Secondly, Catholics, it is said, have a "thing" about authority, which it's best to let them work out in their own way. They *perceive* the world in relations of authority and obedience. Those who are spirited need frequently to *rebel* against authority—to rebel, even, more than to achieve their ends. Rebellion is, if not an end in itself, at least its own vindication. Thus Phil Berrigan's series of battles with his Josephite superiors, and Dan's with Cardinal Spellman and the Jesuits. The heavy authority structure under which priests live calls forth, like abyss to abyss, constant efforts either to show the courage of obedience (Dan goes peaceably to Latin America) or to show the courage of resistance (Dan decides to evade arrest). Every moral struggle is reduced to a struggle against authority. Great strength, clear-sightedness and control are attributed to authorities—direct acts of *no* are interpreted as proofs of manhood. A specifically Catholic syndrome.

Both these explanations have the virtue of explaining one phenomenon of Catholic conduct which is otherwise elusive: the extent to which many Catholics refuse to be judged on the normal utilitarian scale of means and ends that American Protestants and Jews seem to accept as a matter of fact. In a sense, it isn't *winning* (for such Catholics) that counts most; it's giving an accurate and courageous *witness*. There is a kind of long-range pragmatism involved, of course. "Witness" is not a death wish. The whole point of witness is that, ultimately, it generates new life. "Unless the seed fall into the ground and die, it cannot give life."

Dan Berrigan repeats six refrains from St. John of the Cross, then
adds:

> If you wish to become a new man
> You must become a dead man.[1]

Yet I should hasten to draw a contrast. There *is* a powerful
Catholic tradition of witness, not least among the Jesuits in
England or here in the United States among the Indians. But
there is also a strong tradition of pragmatic accommodation, skill-
ful brokerage, and *winning*. Democratic city bosses did not gain
power in this foreign land by acts of "witness." John F. Kennedy,
in actual fact and before legend set in, was a very cautious, pragmatic, hard, ruthless, crisp politician—a gradualist, with all the
sentimentality of gradualism. His great asset was the Harvard and
literary cachet, which enabled him to function as a beguiling
symbol ("style") for those who wanted both the effectiveness of
Richard J. Daley and John Bailey *and* the "culture" of Adlai
Stevenson. (The secret of Robert Kennedy's unique symbolic
power—deeper and more intense, I believe, than John Kennedy's—was that in him *two* Irish Catholic traditions were wed:
the pragmatism of his brother, but a moral passion akin to that of
the Berrigans.)

So I think the two proffered explanations do not go far enough.
There *is* a dramatic, liturgical instinct among Catholics; there *is* a
tradition of rebellion and dissent. But in the United States other
factors are also at work: confusion about "the public," and confusion about "the establishment." For a Catholic, these con-
fusions tend to have special shapes.

Let us suppose that part, at least, of the witness at Catonsville
was intended to "speak to" the American public. *What* was it
trying to say? And to *which* public? The burning of draft files
was a symbolic act. But symbols do not exist outside of history,
abstractly, without reverberation in actual cultures. And the
United States is not one nation but, as Walt Whitman put it, "a
teeming nation of nations." We do not have here one single culture. We are an unassimilated, disunified tangle of cultural his-

tories. No two groups have had exactly the same experience of America.

The word *Catholic* itself—like *Jew*—is an emotive symbol, received differently in different audiences. The word *quota* has a different symbolic history for Jews, Blacks, and Italians. The word *city* has had a different resonance for the Irish, the Scandinavians, the Germans, the British-Americans, the Jews. Symbols of the "law," like traditions of dissent, also differ. Besides ethnic differences (that is, differences in cultural history), there are also regional differences (large cities vs. rural areas; Midwest vs. East; Bible Belt vs. Northeast; etc.).

Maryland was an interesting choice[2] for a major symbolic act connected with war and the military: a "border" state; with a strongly marked Catholic-Protestant antagonism; a state divided by great contrasts between rural and urban attitudes, poverty and affluence, education and cultural simplicity; a state of Anglo-Saxon nativism and strongly defined ethnic enclaves—Greek, Polish, Italian, Black—and all these in a relatively small area.

Is it plausible that the symbol of Catholic priests pouring blood on draft files, or burning draft files with homemade napalm, would have only one, clear meaning to the many publics of Maryland?

Is it likely that the distinction between "violent demonstration" and "nonviolent demonstration" is strong enough in most minds to cut through the power of a prior distinction, that between "legal" and "illegal"? Or through an even more fundamental one: "dramatic, shocking" vs. "conventional" (as when a politician swims in a polluted river—or any of the other publicity stunts seen every evening on television)? A dramatic, shocking illegal act may seem "violent" rather than "nonviolent" to many—and not far different from the nighttime burning of ROTC buildings, churches, or crosses in yards. Whatever the private *intention* of their agents, public symbolic acts are necessarily interpreted according to the hermeneutics supplied by the cultural histories of which they are a part.

There is a difference between (1) the symbolic act whose

purpose is to enhance the integrity of the agent: as if to say, in effect, "I said *no* to the government!" "I've now put my actions where my words are!" "I've lifted a weight of indecision off my chest—I've acted!"[3] And (2) the symbolic act whose jarring is meant to awaken other publics: "Our apologies, good friends, for the fracture of good order, the burning of paper instead of children. . . . We could not, so help us God, do otherwise. For we are sick at heart, our hearts give us no rest for thinking of the Land of Burning Children."[4] And (3) the symbolic act whose purpose is a message to the government: "It was the government who were choosing the victim and the time and place of prosecution. The initiative was entirely in their hands. But in the plan under discussion, the situation was entirely reversed. A few men were declaring that the initiative of action and passion belonged to the peaceable and the resisting."[5] (At Harrisburg, the government had seized the initiative again—generated the accusations and the trial out of its own bosom.)

The last of these alternatives, Daniel Berrigan suggests, is the one by which Philip convinced him to join the others at Catonsville. At first, on reading it, I felt the power of some new insight; but this feeling soon dissolved. The initiative of action and passion *already* belonged to the peaceable and resisting—to counselors, acceptors of draft cards, and the like. What Catonsville did is *raise* the challenge to a frontal, direct level. Catonsville shared in the same vice that marred U.S. policy in Vietnam; it was an escalation down whose future there was no clear limit. Catonsville was a provocation. A generous government might have absorbed it in silence, hearing with equanimity the criticism that would result—just as it often absorbs in silence terrorist acts from the right. (The headquarters of peace movement groups were not infrequently vandalized or symbolically raided.) Catonsville was a wager that the government, like an outraged authority figure, would strike back.

The second alternative—a symbolic act meant to flash the public a signal—is difficult to assess. Even in 1968, a majority or near majority of the population wished to get out of the war in

Vietnam, and even believed that the American entry into the war was "a mistake." Most did not seem to believe that the war was "immoral," or that the United States or Saigon were the sole culpable parties. Most did not believe that this war was different from any other in its brutality to civilians, except that the guerillas persisted in hiding among civilians and there was "nothing to do" except to go after them. Most did not know of the terrors of the air war, which Daniel himself saw firsthand only in February 1968. I am not arguing the merits of these views. But if they approximate the views of most Americans in 1968, would not Catonsville have seemed to most an unbalanced act of unbalanced men?

It takes sophistication of considerable power to understand what the Berrigans intended, to acquire the framework of information within which their action makes sense, and to defend it against even the most obvious objections. By his own admission, Daniel Berrigan, despite three years of antiwar work, was in 1967, when Philip and others first poured blood on draft files, "very far from their understanding of things."[6] It took the Berrigans several days to explain themselves to their warden who was, Daniel writes, "consistently good to us, puzzled as he was by our action, and of a curious integrity, which drove him to question and discuss with us."[7] Not many Americans would have eight days to quiz the symbol-makers about the meaning of their symbol.

It was part of the symbolism, of course, that nice, respectable people were involved: "Neither kooks nor hippies nor rabid Blacks, but imagine! Straight clergy, middle-class, white, religious men and women—what's happening, anyway?"[8]

Perhaps they overestimated the trust most Americans place in other middle-class Americans, even priests. Every day strange sights are seen, absurdities meet the eye. What next?

So the symbolic act was, perhaps, at best a parable, a puzzle, a tease, a torment. It would make people talk. It would make people question. It would not, one might predict, make its agents appear as attractive to all publics as to some. The Berrigans frequently write harsh things ("curious integrity") about ordinary citizens. They write of ordinary Americans with contempt. They seem surprised when the same disgust greets them in return.

Thus the first alternative of the three gains in prominence: There is all too much evidence that the main impetus behind Catonsville was personal need. Daniel describes his feelings the night Philip argued him into committing himself to the Catonsville deed: "Like a shipwreck or a man sucked into quicksand or a drowning man, to whom almost every resource of friendship and ingenuity is lacking, and yet who somehow emerges alive. I say simply that I was saved at the last moment."[9] By Daniel's account, he had had forewarning by letter two weeks earlier, but between dinner and dawn he moved from "bewildered sympathy and shaken readiness" to commitment.

The suddenness of the change bears notice. Daniel stresses how before May 1968 he had "never before" violated a civil law:

We had kept the law, had worked within the law, had believed that change was possible through the law. For many years we had believed that being good Americans was an acceptable secular task; within it we could work out our vocation as Christians. But suddenly, for all of us, the American scene was no longer a good scene. It was, in fact, an immoral scene, corrupted by a useless and wasting war abroad, and a growing, petrifying racism here at home. Ours was a scene that moral men could not continue to approve if they were to deserve the name of men.[10]

But what had so "suddenly" changed in America between, say, 1967 and 1968? The change had been in *them,* in their way of perceiving. America was what it always had been. Only they hadn't noticed it. Racism was not "growing" in America. Manifestly, more was being written and said openly about it, more was being *done* about it, than at any time in the past 350 years. Yes, the war in Vietnam continued. But was that not at least as much due to the ineptitude of the peace movement, unable to translate into political power the desire of a majority or near majority of the public to end the war? Politics was failing America. Surely, the cure for inadequate politics is better politics. Not, of course, if

you're in a hurry, at the end of patience. And not if your aim is
not politics but heaven on earth:

Indeed, the change we underwent was so devastating that one
misses the point entirely if he sees the Catonsville act as merely a protest against this or that aspect of American life. Catonsville, rightly
understood, was a profound 'No' aimed not merely at a federal law
that protects human hunting licenses. Our act was aimed, as our
statement tried to make clear, at every major presumption underlying
American life today. Our act was in the strictest sense a conspiracy;
that is to say, we had agreed together to attack the working assumptions of American life.[11]

One symbolic act meant to challenge the whole history of America? And with what other serviceable history in mind, that of
Ireland?

Next Daniel lists some failures of American institutions. Suppose for a moment that *no* institution, especially a large bureaucratic one, but even a small one like a family, more than one-tenth
fulfills our legitimate expectations of it—always operates at a
level far short of our dreams. Then how do we measure when an
institution is failing a majority of its participants? People cry out
in pain. Catonsville was a cry:

Our act was a denial that American institutions were presently
functioning in a way that good men could approve or sanction. We
were denying that the law, medicine, education, and systems of social
welfare (and above all, the military–para-military styles and objec-
tives that rule and overrule and control these others) were serving the
people, were including the needy, or might be expected to change in
accord with changing needs, that these could enlist or embody the resources of good men—imagination, moral suppleness, pragmatism, or
compassion. We were denying that any major structure of American
life was responding seriously on behalf of the needs of young people,
of black people, of poor people, of working people, of Church people,
of passionate people—as such men scrutinized their institutions,
rightly expecting decent performances of them.[12]

But these are fevered complaints, written in a fevered time.
American institutions today are not in all respects inferior to

those same institutions circa 1890. Banks, corporations, universities, steel mills, law practices, the number of the hungry and destitute, the situation of blacks, the young, medical care—were such institutions or constituencies in *better* shape in 1890, in 1930, in 1955, in 1968?

Does not Scripture tell us that this world belongs to "the Father of lies"? Were we ever led to expect America—or any other empire of Caesar—to be a kingdom of justice, peace, truth, or liberty?

The Berrigans' discovery of evil in the world comes too suddenly, too totally, to engender confidence. Abstractions begin to dance across their pages. "Law and order were violated almost universally. . . . The citizenry were racist, the police were violent, the Congress was delinquent, the courts were conniving, the President was expanding an undeclared war. It went on and on, an interlocking dance of death, a celebration of horror."[13] A painting by Hieronymus Bosch, one of the seven plagues upon Egypt, a timeless portrait of the human condition. But as a political view of politics in America: not very serviceable.

One has the impression of men who had not soon enough taken the measure of evil in the world, or in America, men too soon appalled: the impression of an all-too-American innocence and optimism cruelly shocked into awareness. And of specifically Catholic reactions.

Yet not quite Catholic—a kind of liberal moralism had become in-mixed. Preachiness—and guilt.

The style of social protest in America is largely Protestant: The abolitionists, the Anti-Saloon League, the revival movements of the Bible Belt, the reform movements in American cities. In such movements, moralism ("Tell me once again how evil I am!") is the distinguishing note. Purity is the goal. Struggle is interpreted as war between good and evil (George McGovern on Nixon). The field of action is divided into good guys versus bad guys. George Romney's billboards in New Hampshire: ROMNEY FIGHTS MORAL DECAY. McGovern's: RIGHT FROM THE START. It is as though we should elect, not men who can handle power, but librarians or Boy Scouts. Power and its ambiguities are unmentionable. The Catholic tradition—from Florentine Italy to Dick Daley—is not embarrassed by power, by ambiguity, by realism also about oneself.

A humanistic politics does not have to proceed in the liberal Protestant way. No one showed us better how to resist liberal Protestantism than Reinhold Niebuhr. It is quite possible to work for reforms (or even revolution) in a way that does not identify the good with one's own side, evil with the other side. It is quite possible to stress the fact that, in politics, issues are not purely and simply moral, but rather embedded in institutional inertia and social necessities that require patient, organic political ways and skills, as well as sound moral insight, a sharp eye for interests and powers as well as longings for a better world.

The left is skilled at diagnosing the totalism and complacence of the warmakers: how "pragmatism" led Dean Rusk to speak of "our" side and the "other side"; how good came to be identified with America, evil with Hanoi; how wisdom and justice and modesty came to be violated in an excess of clarity, zeal, and ideology. The left is not so skilled in noting that its own descriptions of *its* enemies—the warmakers—share in exactly the same simplemindedness, repeat exactly the same dehumanization, represent the same fever of ideological purity.[14]

Perhaps one should say that *all* of us live in a radically evil world, now, as always, under the sway of forces of deceit. "The plague," as Camus says, "is in all of us." Where is there on this earth a place in which to escape from participation in the general evil? What Daniel writes of America could be said—altering the local accusations—of the English, the French, the Italians, the Swedes, the North Vietnamese; no human society being without hereditary and institutionalized evil. Too easily the world is divided into the children of light and the children of darkness:

Redeem the times! The times are inexpressibly evil. *Christians* pay conscious—indeed religious—tribute to Caesar and Mars: by approval of overkill tactics, by brinksmanship, by nuclear liturgies, by racism, by support of genocide. *They* embrace their society with all their heart, and abandon the cross. *They* pay lip service to Christ and military service to the powers of death. And yet, and yet, the times are inexhaustibly good, solaced by the courage and hope of *many.* The truth rules, Christ is not forsaken. In a time of death, *some men—* the *resisters, those who work hardily for social change, those who preach and embrace the unpalatable truth*—such men overcome death, their lives are bathed in the light of the resurrection, the truth has set them free. In the jaws of death, of contumely, of good and ill report, they proclaim their love of the brethren. [*Italics supplied.*][15]

Political judgments are not so easy. On the one side the somnolent, on the other men "bathed in the light of the Resurrection." Berrigan does not perceive the class bias he embodies: a vision of good and evil proper to the upper classes and their children versus a vision on the part of ordinary citizens of lesser education but no less intelligence and good faith. A struggle between the Berrigans and their class versus other classes in America.

It is the lack of "normalcy" that troubles Daniel. Fevers, cries, tears, flounderings, despairs. How to keep evil away from ourselves? How to be pure? How, indeed, to find a purpose for life, excitement, the razor's edge of awareness, "the mind's edge honed"? Among those whom the jading of everyday stifles, whose economic problem is solved, for whom life means "self-fulfillment and growth," who are impatient with what others find the inevitable intractability of life.

We have chosen to say, with the gift of our liberty, if necessary of our lives, the violence stops here, the death stops here, the suppression of the truth stops here, the war stops here. We wish also to place in question by this act all suppositions about normal times, longings for an untroubled life in a somnolent church, that neat timetable of ecclesiastical renewal which, in respect to the needs of men, amounts to another form of time serving.[16]

If Daniel Berrigan had been living a settled life, sights well established, in an institutional setting in which he felt at home, how different these words would look. Instead, he himself tells us of his years of restlessness—rootlessness, even—traveling, searching, experimenting. Normalcy is—has long been—an affront to him. It is not unfair to wonder how much being a priest in this troubled era, in an order long on its stress on utter obedience; being celibate; and being without either a life-plan or a settled future has to do with it. Thousands of other priests and sisters are simultaneously experiencing great personal upheavals. To many, their own normalcy fractured by the times, normalcy is a "disease."

I think of the good, decent, peace-loving people I have known by the thousands, and I wonder. How many of them are so afflicted with *the wasting disease of normalcy* that, even as they declare for the peace, their hands out with an instinctive spasm in the direction of their loved ones, in the direction of their comforts, their home, their security, their income, their future, their plans—that five-year plan of studies, that ten-year plan of professional status, that twenty-year plan of family growth and unity, that fifty-year plan of decent life and honorable natural demise. "Of course, let us have the peace," we cry, "but at the same time let us have normalcy, let us lose nothing, let our lives stand intact, let us know neither prison nor ill repute nor disruption of ties." [*Italics supplied.*][17]

Suppose, however, that obtaining peace in Vietnam is not a matter of resistance or going to jail. Suppose it depends upon the much harder task of building a political coalition strong enough to *institutionalize* a new direction for the country—not to dream about it, but to execute the dream? In the poor, clumsy, inadequate way of institutions, no doubt. In politics, one does not expect immediate success, and surely not complete success. But there is no substitute for organizing, persuading, taking the long, slow march toward political power. Such a path requires faith in the nation, in its institutions, and in its people. It also requires roots. Daniel knows something about roots. He identifies his own:

I believe a man's possibility is in large part measured by the tradition he comes out of. I have said it repeatedly on the Cornell campus; I have said it before the SDS, before the religious communities, before the fraternities, before my own soul; like it or not, we are what we

have been. A man can claim to be going somewhere only if he has
come from somewhere. Alienation in any absolute sense can only be
a source of dislocation and irresponsibility. To go somewhere, a man
must come from somewhere. For myself, if my claim to Christian
tradition is valid, it is so only because I am trying to embody that
conception of citizenship and faith that runs from Jesus to Paul to
Galileo to Newman to Teilhard to Pope John to myself.[18]

And Daniel also knows his family's roots:

We came out of a kind of northern Appalachian poverty. In the
thirties our family was a rural one, a part of the pandemic poverty
of the great depression years. And we barely made it. We learned
firsthand the near catastrophe of the "crash," the harsh, slow recovery of the Roosevelt years, the first moves toward social reform.
We were the hands into which the New Deal was dealt. Public relief
programs, the Civilian Conservation Corps, the Industrial Reconstruction Act; we ate our alphabet soup and were grateful for it,
however thin it was drawn. During those same years, while federal
institutions were shaken to their foundations, another fact of life
surrounded my family. We were members of a church whose main
word, whether we or others liked it or not, was revolutionary.[19]

Yet Daniel seems astonishingly without social roots—not close
to his parents' world, not close to their friends, or to the seventy
or eighty million other Americans who share a world like theirs.
He praises his parents for their daily goodness, their understanding, their resistance to the bitch-goddess of status and success.
Otherwise, for years he has been living in another world. Again
and again, in *The Geography of Faith* Robert Coles tries to bring
Daniel to even a moment's sympathy for lower-middle-class
whites. Daniel can't even hear the words. Changes the subject.
Nothing. Zero. It is absolutely astonishing.

Daniel's understanding of immigrant history is stillborn. He is
as alienated from his own history as a Black trying to straighten
his hair. One of the few sentences Daniel gives to the subject is a
pallid piece of ideology at best: "Catholics in large numbers
came to this country relatively late and came as large 'ethnic'
groups, each impoverished and frightened and *essentially ori-*

ented toward winning its own place in the sun; for these reasons I
think social and political radicalism could not take root." [Italics
supplied.][20] Millions of Catholics are hardly a generation away
from men and women in their own families who were fired from
their jobs, jailed, beaten, and murdered for their union activities
or in the struggles to survive in a hostile society. Why the historical amnesia? These traditions are not dead, they await the breath
of living leadership.

"But in the late twentieth century," Daniel writes, "the Catholic community is thoroughly a part of the American social and
economic and political scene—hence we have a corresponding
obligation to look outward, extend ourselves, reach across national and racial and ideological barriers."[21] Charity, goes the
old saw, begins at home. So desperately needy are the Italian-
Americans of Newark and Canarsie, the Poles of Detroit and
Buffalo, the Irish of Queens, the lower-middle-class Jews of Forest
Hills and Williamsburg—needy in spirit, needy in political power
and purpose, needy in identity and roots and goals. They are not
nearly so secure in status as Daniel imagines, nor has their
economic problem been solved—they do not have the liberties
involved in university life, the trips to France, to Eastern Europe,
and indeed to Hanoi. They do not have summer homes, or friends
in publishing and the arts. Since 1954, Daniel has been rising in
class and status and "sophistication," but millions of others
remain where he was then. Most of them are like his parents, no
better, no worse.

The harshest way to put what I am saying is that Daniel and
Philip have become Uncle Toms. Their words about their own
people—Catholic, immigrant, Irish—are characteristically harsh,
with a distancing quality that informs the reader: "We're beyond
that." Otherwise, indifference. They concentrate on the sons and
daughters of the educated classes, the college-goers: resisters,
Weathermen, movement people. They fail to see the accumula-
tions of class and status and education and income generally
required as an admissions ticket into "the movement." They fail
to see that the peculiar self-hatred and despair characteristic of

"the movement"—Daniel often speaks of his flock as wounded, hurt, despairing, torn by hopelessness and powerlessness—are precisely the fruit of social rank. The "best and brightest" brought on the war (Daniel has learned a little about hereditary Anglo-Saxon wealth and power at Cornell), and now their children suffer spasms of guilt. *Of course* the professional classes are afflicted with self-hatred. *They* were managing this society, and as recently as the days of John F. Kennedy and John Kenneth Galbraith they were telling us that America, this "affluent society," *had* no problems technical skills could not solve—*their* particular technical skills.

I share—have shared for years—Daniel and Philip's suspicion of "liberal intellectuals." (A useful exercise: circle in their books Daniel's and Philip's use of the word *liberal*. Pejorative nearly always.) It is part of an American Catholic inheritance, shared by all immigrant Catholics, even when they themselves are liberal. So much fraudulence and hypocrisy, such complacence and doublethink fly under that standard. Catholics know about liberal fraudulence as penetratingly as Blacks know it, and for similar reasons: liberal intellectuals on the whole are probably even more anti-Catholic than they are (in the depths of their hearts) anti-Black. Daniel Berrigan's analysis of professors and administrators at Cornell, in *No Bars to Manhood,* has the edge and bite of an outsider, no member of the club, fed by historical resentments he is not even fully conscious of. (Not by accident was so high a percentage of radical students, particularly of the tone-setters, Catholic and Jewish.) "I have a distrust of leading people," Daniel tells Robert Coles.

On the other hand, Berrigan idealizes his own constituency—"certain youths, certain blacks, certain poor people," as Robert Coles delicately puts it. There was a radical fever on American campuses in the late 1960s. To a large extent, that fever was self-serving. As the draft was ended, protest declined astonishingly. Cries of "revolution" were fun, but when those in power took them seriously and acted accordingly, revolutionaries seemed surprised and affronted, as if to say: "That's not fair." Year after year, members of the movement found excuse after excuse *not* to go to the people (as Ho Chi Minh had gone to *his* people), to live among them and to persuade, and to build a political machine that would turn political institutions around. Daniel speaks lightly about his own methods: "a raw kind of fundamentalism," a "thousand-year project." "What we are really searching for are the many valuable things that must be done if a very complex society like ours [how seldom he even indicates its complexity!] is to be reborn again—made humane, rendered less paralyzed by its obsessions and fears and conceits."[22] But while we wait a thousand years for the fulfillment of *that* project, what about the bursts of impatience that led to Catonsville—that "end of a long patience" he spoke of—after his sudden conversion?[23]

The time scheme is quite confused. Is it truly sensible to reject the slow, lumbering ways of democratic politics because there isn't time, and then to commend the Vietnamese thousand-year patience until the nation is made humane? It is a priest talking, not a politician. Categories of politics and categories of humanism have become confused. No doubt, integrity demands a unity of politics and humanism in the same person and in society. But to demand of political institutions (or political acts) more than they can supply is no ministry of peace. To interpret structural, institutional problems as though they were problems of spiritual sickness is to put matters backwards.

Even when a majority of Americans *opposed* the war, they could not force the president to end it. The American Constitution has a radical flaw not found in the parliamentary system of England: our president is not strictly accountable, week by week, either to the opposition or to the press. There is no effective check on an executive war. We have got to create such a check.

To turn swiftly, instead, as Philip (rather than Daniel) tends to do, to the deficiencies of capitalism and to invoke the need for socialism is not illuminating. The grossness of American economic practices in Latin America unquestionably needs drastic revision. Our political system has not, so far, proved very successful in separating corporate economic powers from the political

powers of the state. How to discipline economic power is, unquestionably, the profoundest problem of a humanistic ethic. Does
one accomplish that end by burning draft papers at Catonsville?

On the one hand, the defendants tell us, all we did was burn a
few pieces of paper. On the other hand, they tell us, we challenged the whole system of law and all the assumptions of American history. We said *no* to the system.

Politically speaking, what they did is to give the self-doubt and
self-hatred of the educated classes—"the best and the brightest"—precedence over any other cultural needs. For what is
called "the system" is managed by the educated classes—the
readers of books, subscribers to magazines, patrons of universities. It is to one segment of this new class, it appears, that the
themes of "the movement," the counterculture and the New Left
appealed most. It is this segment that Daniel and Philip felt it
important to be out "in front" of, to have credibility in, to give
leadership to.

The self-image of this class is that it is uniquely composed of
enlightened men and women of virtue, humanism, courage,
caring. It does not take much analysis to show, however, that each
of its purported virtues promotes its own self-interest. The new
class has vested interests in change. As a class, its stock-in-trade is
change in life-styles and living habits and technical needs, on
which it makes its living. It has a vested interest in social and
political change. As a class, its most marketable skill is organizing and managing people. It has a vested interest in an alliance
between activist whites and activist Blacks (rather than, say, an
alliance between working whites and working Blacks). As a class,
its only hope of outvoting "Middle America" is the nurturing of a
"new coalition of change" among (as it imagines) the poor, the
Black, the young, and "women." (As if all women shared the
views of some women of the new class.) It has a vested interest in
the shock value of selected atrocities in Vietnam and elsewhere—
to discredit other American establishments with which it wrestles
for power.

For there is not one "establishment" in the United States.

There are at least three: northeastern money, Sun Belt money and northeastern communications. The last-named has most sympathy for "the movement." Daniel Berrigan gives ample witness in his writings that his own main ambience is that of professional people, people in the arts, publishing people, people in communications. It is important to note the new wealth and power accumulated in this segment of the population over the last thirty years, with the advent of television, the paperbook book, phonographic equipment, and the growing ranks of economically dependent youths nourished in the media through twentyhood. The sense of reality in this class is increasingly electronic. It has its own consciousness and ways of perceiving. It celebrates itself as the wave of the future, the bearer of a new humanism.

Neither Daniel nor Philip shows himself to be very prophetic in relation to *that* culture. They seem to be to a large extent voices *of* that culture. But not only a culture: a class, a power group, an interest group, a rising and ambitious establishment, arrogant toward those who disagree with it, divisive in its impact on American society, moralistic in its foreign-policy preachments, blind to its own power, interests and corruptions. In a word, an interest group like any other, melioristic and humane in some ways, destructive in others.

The sense in which I judge Daniel and Philip Berrigan to be *morally* wrong in their actions inheres in the same sense in which I see in their actions a certain moral beauty and power. It is not quite enough to say that they did in act what they spoke in speech (the new class values that accomplishment much too highly)— Nazi soldiers and Ku Klux Klansmen have also had the courage to act as they believed. "The courage to act": a Nietzschean motif, capable of mutually cancelling uses. Often it has been used as a battlecry against democrats and liberals, who quite purposefully interpose procedures between speech and action, quite cheerfully make themselves vulnerable to charges of timidity and pallid reasonableness. Daniel frequently invokes images of "manhood" and "hero." "The heroic man has been pulled down in our times—there are so few models of manhood allowed."[24] But there are many kinds of courage, many kinds of hero. The large, bold action of dreams is not always an action to be trusted. It is often in Bonhoeffer's phrase, "one of the underlying themes of tragedy."

The morality of an action springs also from many other sources. With Robert Coles, I find at least two springs of Daniel's actions inadequate: his estimation of the persistence of evil in human beings, in institutions, and in history is far too shallow (hence his constant need to promote hope, optimism, joyousness; his grasping at straws and signs); and his estimation of both the specific evil and specific intransigence of contemporary American society. Long before the sudden enlightenment of the Berrigans, American society was far more involved in murder, exploitation, cruelty, and injustice than its own propaganda indicated. Camus made the same point about France. There is hereditary injustice written into every institution in every human society. Nowhere is the social order just, equal, free, humane, truthful—except by some relative standard. Nowhere does the society of actuality coincide with the society of dreams.

Even in his earlier poetry, Daniel found it difficult to accept the human condition. Always the attempt to fly away—and the metal wire on the leg holding the hawk down. For a time, he celebrated the bite of reality, like Gerard Manley Hopkins in "The Wind-hover." But as he rose in his actual professional state, he became more and more restless, without roots or ties or culturally defined limits. He sought the infinite. (It is a word Coles, too, feels constrained to use: "You are almost *infinitely* more optimistic than I am.")[25] Daniel craves excitement, adventure, new tests for his spirit. He often complains of having felt dead, half-alive, stifled, decaying—and he regularly seeks new acts of courage to restore his sense of "being on the edge."[26] Great spirits, great explorers, often feel impelled to break new ground. But it is important—at least in politics—to distinguish carefully between one's own need for the heroic and one's people's needs. In poetry, in philosophy, in the spiritual life it is proper, in the name of all, to plumb the depths. To bring that sort of adventure into the

realm of practical politics is the specific temptation of the artist
and the priest; it is a grievous moral danger both to the agent and
to the people. To do so in the name of nonviolence offers, at least,
some safeguard. But to do so as a leader of "a movement" and in
order to stay out "in front," to imagine that "finding points of
hope" is a political act, is to mislead, to engender false hopes, to
breed illusions.

Martin Luther King, Jr., by contrast, was indeed a political
leader with a political program. He had a strategy. He worked
outside of established political channels, as an innovator. But he
accepted both full political responsibility for and clear political
measurement of what he was doing. He acted always for specific
political gains, on carefully limited and selected targets. He *knew
what he wanted* from each act.

Gandhi, too, had a political method, a clearly drawn constituency, a program, a political goal. His methods, too, were unconventional, deeply rooted in the spiritual life of himself and his
people. But he knew that politics is responsibility for power;
politics is organization; politics is accountability. He founded a
party, launched a nation, cast out an armed imperial force.

A plain lack of political direction and political substance
makes the politics of the Berrigans seem apolitical. It seems like a
politics of resentment, anger, desperation—but not a politics
going any place in particular, creating a constituency, fulfilling a
larger program. Improvisatory, temperamental, fitful, yet astonishingly far-flung and (in a manner of speaking) coordinated,
and steeped in traditions of generosity and self-sacrifice, the
protests of the Catholic left—"the Boston Two, the Baltimore
Four, the Catonsville Nine, the Milwaukee Fourteen, the Washington Nine, the New York Eight"—seemed to function as cries
out across the night from lonely spirits to lonely spirits, aimed at
bringing cheer and consolation, hope, the semblance even of
movement to "the movement." No doubt these were heroic acts,
for which a real price in real lives was paid and is being paid. No
doubt in the grand calculus of public opinion and its impact on
the makers of decisions, these actions were not without fruit. No

doubt they rescued the battered name of Catholicism from too
much conformity, from impassivity and hardness of heart—
added counters to the scale dangling opposite the lower scale
marked "Spellman and Vietnam." No doubt, a legend was born
to history, which future generations of conservative bishops will
offer as comfort to eager questioners: "Even then, you see, the
Church was not without its heroes."

But in comparison with King or Gandhi, the politics of the
Berrigans is deracinated, offers no promise of political change,
whether reformist or revolutionary. Philip himself told Francine
Gray just before the trial at Harrisburg began:

You become increasingly modest about the effects that any action
can have on the monolith of the American empire. [*Monolith?*
America is so diverse! That's what baffles changemakers.] You
have to draw some conclusions about what social change people
want. . . . The record proves that they don't want very much. [Has
any nation in history more willingly undergone relentless, annual
social change?] I used to have a hopeful view of resources in church
or in student coalitions, or in minority group militants. This hope
was unfounded. We found these coalitions had no roots, that they
died like a desert flower, bloomed and died overnight, that there
was no space for them to get any roots. . . . I have absolutely no
regrets about what I have done, and no regrets about doing it twice.
But would I do it again? Probably not.[27]

In the end, the many acts of dramatic rebellion seemed aimed
at recreating the feeling of vital faith. In the end, the politics of
Catonsville did not add up to the joyousness of that most beau-
tiful of trials, the trial of the Catonsville Nine; it ended in the
shame and misery of Harrisburg: petty, embarrassing, as hum-
bling as Isaiah 53 might have specified. In the end "at the edge"
comes to mean, perhaps, "the edge of sadness." The smile, the
joy, the pixie wit of Daniel always seemed forced, Christian joy
willed into existence across the face of terror. Suffering not
unknown to him. Stretches of emptiness beyond description.

Rebellion was, so many lines in the documents suggest, a sur-
rogate for faith, a seeking for faith, a searching for the edges of

the world where faith might be restored again, the probing for a mission. Not a political program, rather a probe for personal authenticity, a journey into doubt and despair. "My brother," Dan tells Coles, "wants to live 'on the edge,' so to speak; he wants to live with all kinds of ironies and absurdities."[28] But why? Does a man deliberately tempt the Holy Spirit? Is it a kind of vocation? Something happens to those in such a predicament,

. . . and maybe the "something" has to do with *the development of consciousness*—that could be one way of putting it. It seems fairly certain, as far as one can be certain in very obscure times, that like it or not my brother and I are involved in a struggle *for a certain kind of moral awareness*; and it also seems that the moral questions we are trying to raise cannot be raised in the traditional way—at a polite "debate" or in a "discussion" at a "forum." I am *in jeopardy* and it is from such a position that I hope to discuss and use moral issues. [*Italics supplied.*][29]

Such a luxury it seems. Such a personal test—like a stunt driver, speedcar racer, mountain climber. Our professional, rootless classes experience a certain deadness in their lives. Many seek to test themselves, morally.

Thus a new form of the Ignatian *Spiritual Exercises*. Precipitate a spiritual crisis: thirty days in jail or three months in hiding. Accept humiliation. Silence, prayer, and meditation. Physical abuse. Torments of the imagination. Purifications of the soul. It is an effective novitiate for humanistic living. If normal living has not brought you through the terrifying experiences of nothingness, try opposition to the government. See how the nation looks, from the bottom up. An exercise in perception.

In a measure, for a remnant, it is a form of politics. In the atomization of academic life (now that education belongs not merely to the gentlemanly sons and ladylike daughters of a small elite but to eight million of the offspring of the middle class and even of the poor); in the bureaucratization of the great professions; and in the isolation of the relatively novel and surely un-Catholic nuclear family—in *all* these dreadful modern circumstances, there are bruised and vulnerable persons whose hope requires nurture, whose despair begs for consolation. Not least because they were brought up to expect, not the cross, not absurdity, not the daily bread of despair—but a world of lawns and hedges, reason, buoyancy, and optimism. They were born little liberals. Nobody prepared them for how ugly the world is. They always got their way.

The fury of the disappointed knows no bounds. The rage of those who believe themselves both innocent and omnipotent— able to bring instant peace and justice—has been amply demonstrated in America. Many have discovered an ordinary human impotence, and some have discovered their own lack of innocence. Daniel himself recalls a conference on pacifism in which a silent participant was at last prevailed upon to let the others hear his thoughts: "I believe there is enough latent violence in this room to start a war."[30]

And among guilt-stricken members of the privileged classes, what sudden adulation of victims, glorification of victims, what status was conferred upon those lucky enough to be victims and therefore innocent. Ah, to be Black—or to stand among the Vietnamese (North)—or to be a convict, a criminal—every utterance of a victim vatic—every sentiment a mysterious marvel. Yes, here, too, a ministry worthy of the Curé d'Ars or the humble priest of Bernanos' *Diary*. Here the solid good sense of a priest— triply blessed with a good, tough Irish father, a Depression childhood, and a Jesuit novicemaster—could be of inestimable value. A ministry desperately needed.

Add to these factors those circles of the secular where word of Simone Weil and worker priests and the Gospels as revolution had not gone out—where the deserts of pragmatism had at last awakened the thirst for conscience, for transcendence, and even for absolutes: *moral, immoral; right, wrong*. Ministry enough here, too, ministry for a thousand men: "One does what one is called upon to do. . . . I feel responsible for a very small area of life. I can only do what I can do."[31]

A priest, perhaps even more than other humans in a time like ours, is authenticated by what he *does*. Many priests need to prove that the words they say leap from deeds. If a deed can be imagined as heroic, good, and maybe even necessary ("I feel stronger than ever that the whole thing is extremely important"), then I—above all—must not shrink from trying it. Before my flock does, I must test the way.

Then the very Irishness of it. ("Irish" is the nickname Philip gave to Sister Elizabeth McAlister.) The fighting Irish. Contentious—loving a good scrap. Think of Pat Moynihan and Andrew Greeley—or Jimmy Breslin's habitual vein of pugnacity. "Always causin' trouble." Daniel speaks of:

the political consequences of being human beings at a time when the fate of people, of the world, demanded that one not be merely a listener, or a good friend, but yes, *be in trouble.* So, in a way I can only be thankful that my life has edged over to the point that I am now simply, publicly, churchwise, society-wise *an outsider, a troublemaker,* a condemned man. I say that, I hope and pray, not to be arbitrary, or romantic, or self-serving in a dramatic way, but in order to respond to a reading of the times, as Bonhoeffer tried to read the times. [*Italics supplied.*][32]

An Irish way of reading *any* time.

It is not politics, then, that the Berrigans—Daniel, at least—are up to. What the radical man "is finally looking for is not a solution (knowing as he does that human history has not offered solutions). He is really working for a creation: a new man in a new society."[33] A new way of preaching the gospel. Not from the pulpit but from the jail; not peaceably giving to Caesar what is Caesar's, but dramatically saying *no* when Caesar's active fingers grasp even what is God's. Such a new mode is not inauthentic. And in the suffering it brings, in the exposure of faults and weaknesses, in the possibilities for grievous error, a burning and pure faith may also be found: perhaps, by an irony, *not* where one looked, and yet even in the *mistake,* generous as it was, of looking there. ("It was more important to have explored this track than not to have.")[34] So the good man is protected on both sides, whether he was wrong, or whether he was correct. Thus grace outwits even the tragedy that Bonhoeffer discerns, when one has chosen the lesser of two evils and that turns out to be the worse.

Not for nothing, nonetheless, did Maritain warn us about danger of the clergyman's judgment in politics. True, the priest is a citizen like any other. But the Church is not the world, the cleric is not the layman, the laws of politics are not yet, at any rate, not by a long shot—those of the Gospels. The radical man—or at least the radical priest—may be working for "the new man in the new society." But the man of politics cannot wait for that far-off blessed coming. He must plan for the old man in the old society, that old world deeply imprinted in the heart of the New World. (History's greatest piece of ideology: that metaphor of innocence: New World!)

Every life dramatizes presuppositions. The drama I find my own life living out includes two elementary presuppositions different from Daniel's. Daniel is Teilhardian in a way I cannot be: "I believe," he tells Coles, "that it is entirely possible that the first instance of *a really great breakthrough* is going to take place in America." And again: "I don't accept the inevitability of, in a religious sense—" Coles interrupts: "Of original sin?" Berrigan again: "Okay. Or let's say its omnipresent hold over human institutions." Coles: "You think man can be better than he has been in the past or appears to be now?" Berrigan: "Well, I would put it like this: I think there has not yet been a *real revolution.*"[35]

The revolution, it is true, is moral or not at all (Péguy). But there has not yet been a real revolution. And will not be. The human condition is no excuse for inaction; the human condition *includes* our responsibility to act and to diminish, at least by a little, the number of those who suffer. But one will not be so inclined to extremes of hope and despair—and one will understand better the Vietnamese reflections on patience, which sound utterly out of keeping with Daniel's political impatience—if one grants very little to the myth of history, the myth of progress.

Daniel writes, incredibly to me, of moral progress: "It is up to growing children to surpass the moral understanding and the world-awareness of their parents, and further rid us of the ves-

tiges of violence and racism and the rest."[36] *Vestiges* of violence
and racism, he says, during the most violent heavy bombing in all
of history. Are we not all children of parents, and are we in our
generation—we who make our mark in the world—morally supe-
rior to *our* parents? Will our children be better than we? Ah,
watching the college generation I do not believe it. "We blew it!"
Captain America says in *Easy Rider* for the generation of four
years ago, and for every generation.

So if we can be redeemed, it isn't here. A vale of tears, the
prayer of Our Lady called it. Nothing in the experience of the
twentieth century proves otherwise. Daniel, I sometimes believe,
lives from a vein of liberal optimism that has little to do with
Christianity.

Secondly, politics is not the realm of salvation. It is a realm *in*
which humans, concentrating on something else, do save their
souls or lose them. But those who seek in politics the meaning of
life are doomed to frustration. Politics is far from being able to
fulfill the capacities of the human soul. Politics is the field of
power, interests, and institutional arrangements. It offers a
grubby, demanding, unsatisfying, exhausting way of life—and
even those who like it, who are made for it, suffer occupational
distortions the best of them are the first to mock. If the state is a
ship, politics is the stinking boiler room.

Better perhaps: politics is the flesh in which the Gospels are,
however inadequately, incarnate. The Christ does not come as a
"real revolution" or "the first instance of a really great breakthrough." He comes despised by those who expect more, in a
guise altogether too ordinary, too encased in the weaknesses flesh
is heir to—including political systems. Were there not slaves in
the Roman Empire? Was there then no stench of racism? Was
violence to wait until America came to be?

Still more to the point: seventy million people from whom the
Berrigans spring have, just as surely as Dan's and Phil's parents,
goodness in them, political energy and political wisdom. It is a
vast, neglected constituency. And who speaks for them today?
Not George McGovern, Lord knows, but not Richard Nixon

either. Not George Meany, but not General Walker, either. Not
Jesse Jackson, but not Governor Maddox. Nor are they Archie
Bunkers (Bunker being, after all, a classy Anglo-Saxon name).
Their economic problems are not solved. Less than 5 percent of
the people in this nation make over $25,000 per year. Seventy-
five percent do not make as much as $15,000. Well, try to educate
four or five children on $15,000 a year, with as much as 25
percent or 30 percent going into various taxes, another hefty
percentage accounting for fierce inflation since 1945—you will
find yourself not far above and perhaps below the minimum
standard of living for a family of four (not six) in New York
City, and not eligible for scholarships or other forms of assistance.

When Daniel assaults the family as an instrument of the state,
let him recall the immigrant traditions of the extended family and
the functioning neighborhood: not the isolated, demoralized family of the fully Americanized middle classes. Though millions still
retain these traditions, millions of others cannot now return to
them. But we can reinforce a new version of such ancient and
wise ways of life today, *if* we develop a system of social rewards
for interfamily and neighborhood cooperation, in child care and
in the many tasks of schooling, in job apprenticeship, in health
care, in care for the elderly and in other vital economic functions.

Let Daniel look into the history of radicalism in his family and
in millions of other immigrants' families—and discharge from his
mind the self-hatred it was the business of Americanizers to
spread among us, the idea (for one) that our forebears were so
self-centered they yielded no room to radicalism. Where did such
progressive politics as we have had in these last one hundred
immigrant years find its power—in the Republican party? Were
Sacco and Vanzetti Boston Brahmins, think you?

At Harrisburg, the Berrigans were surprised by the good sense
of the jury. "Never underestimate the people," Philip Berrigan
wrote exultantly. "Their common sense usually prevails against
the excesses of government."[37] Why does this sentiment come so
late? Why, then, his earlier gloom about social change in this

most mobile, changing nation on earth? Why not a greater sensitivity to a vast people of varying styles and experiences, and deep longing to make America work: and work morally, too?

Didn't the Berrigans know—or care to find out—that the lower middle class were, like the poor, sending a disproportionate number of sons to a puzzling and unwanted war? Didn't they know that workers hated the war, even if for reasons of class they hated war protesters, too? Were they so out of touch with their people that they did not see how radical politics—in its glib accusations of "white racism"—has its own form of bigotry, stereotypes people in manichaean fashion, polarizes, divides, embitters?

Do they not recognize that the price of 250 years of slavery and another century of racism is not being paid by those who instituted it, but cleverly shifted to the shoulders of those who themselves can scarcely endure the worsening burdens of the northern cities, liberated from serfdom only as few decades back as Blacks from slavery?

Don't they appreciate the good will and groping generosity of working people, if only they will not, on top of their other burdens, be *penalized* for integrating their neighborhoods and schools—penalized by realtors, bankers, educators, insurance companies, and even by the media, as they now most assuredly are. For if this *is* a nation racist in its institutions, more than moral exhortations—more than burnt draft files—are needed. The system of punishments laid upon working class people, Black and white, must be altered. The perception of these problems might well be unitive, not divisive: through lenses of class, not alone through lenses of race.

Now there is in all this ample room for political organizing, articulation and creation, plenty of outlet for moral and political energy.

It is, I suppose, the contempt Daniel and Philip seem to have had for the very people whence they spring—uneducated, working class, hard-pressed, unchampioned, unspoken for, much disdained—that makes me conclude, in the end, that despite the memory of the flames in that basket at Catonsville which all of us and our children will cherish, their example was neither moral nor political in the full dimensions our nation had need of. What they did served the already saved, an educated elite. It was romantic. It was the expression of a personal quest. It was clerical. It lacked political penetration and point. For too many it was repellent rather than persuasive. In all these ways, it was morally and politically deficient.

Yet for many, on a cold night, it offered beauty enough to warm their hands at. In a dry season, the Catholic tradition and the American imagination were nourished.

"Imagine, would ye, two Irish *priests!* One a Jesuit. Upped th' establishment pretty good, don't you think?"

It satisfied a certain American Catholic resentment, in a bold and Catholic gesture of self-sacrifice.

NOTES

1. *The Dark Night of Resistance* (New York: Doubleday, 1971), p. 51. Members of the Cornell SDS said: "Catonsville was not politically serious, it was *machismo*, romantic." To which Daniel countered: "The New Left suffers from American pragmatism. . . . It fights violence with the tools of violence, I fight it with the Gandhian and Christian dimensions of nonviolence. They measure effectiveness by pragmatic results, I see it as immeasurable, as the impact of symbolic action. The New Left only stresses political activity, I would like to be more classical and Greek, I am like Socrates choosing jail, choosing the *ideal.*" See Francine Gray, *Divine Disobedience* (New York: Alfred A. Knopf, 1970), p. 140. Which acts will be remembered longer—those of Cornell's SDS, or those of Catonsville? But besides these two types of effectiveness, there is a third: the creation of enduring institutions, or the revivification of ancient ones. Three types of pragmatism, which interact.

2. Shock value and insult figured in the choice of Catonsville. Francine Gray reports: "The month of May was spent scanning the Baltimore area for the right draft board. The little town of Catonsville, eight miles north of downtown Baltimore, was chosen because it was a sitting duck, and highly symbolic. Catonsville was a lily-white, middle-class suburban town of smug brick houses and pleasant oak-lined streets, a Maryland version of Larchmont or Purchase. 'We loved the idea of hitting that kind of

conservative, racist community,' Mische says. 'We loved to hit them with an action not performed by hippies but by college graduates, three of them clerics, all nicely dressed in white collars or in suits and ties.' " *Divine Disobedience*, p. 130.

3. Daniel told the Court: "I was realizing at Cornell that one simply could not announce the Gospel from his pedestal . . . when he was not down there sharing the risks and burdens and the anguish of his students, whose own lives were placed in the breech by us, by this generation that I and others belong to. I saw suddenly, and it struck me with the force of lightning, that my position was false, that I was threatened with verbalizing my moral substance out of existence. That I was placing upon young shoulders the filthy burden of the original sin of war. That I, too, was asking them to become men in a ceremony of death. At that point I realized that, although I was too old to carry a draft card, there were other ways of getting into trouble with a state totally intent upon war . . . that one could not stop within the law while the moral, social condition deteriorated . . . structures of compassion breaking down, neighborhoods slowly rotting, the poor slowly despairing, social unrest forever present in the land, especially among the young people, who are our only hope, our only resource." He spoke then of a sixteen-year-old boy in Syracuse who had burned himself in protest against the war. Daniel visited him in the hospital. "The boy was lying in total torment upon his bed, and his body looked like a piece of meat that had been cast upon a grill. He died very shortly thereafter, but I felt that my sense had been invaded in a new way, and that I had understood again the power of death in the modern world, and that I must speak of this and act in the opposite direction. . . . So I went to Catonsville. And I burned some paper because I was trying to say that the burning of children was inhuman and unbearable, and, as Brother Darst said, a cry is the only response. . . . I did not want the children or the grandchildren of the jury to be burned with napalm." Ibid., pp. 199–200.

4. *Night Flight to Hanoi* (New York: Macmillan, 1968), p. xvi.

5. *No Bars to Manhood* (New York: Bantam, 1971), p. 15.

6. Ibid., p. 14.

7. Ibid., p. 16.

8. Ibid., p. 41.

9. Ibid., pp. 14–15.

10. Ibid., p. 40.

11. Ibid.

12. Ibid.

13. Ibid., p. 42.

14. Berrigan describes for Robert Coles "the Manichaean madhouse":

"Our society declares itself good and virtuous in principle and declares others (minorities within the nation and various countries on the several continents) to be the enemy. We don't want to 'live and let live'; we want to dominate." *The Geography of Faith* (Boston: Beacon Press, 1971), p. 162. Daniel's own declarations about *his* enemies—General Hershey, J. Edgar Hoover, somnolent Christians, etc.—seldom give *them* credit for seeing some things more clearly than he and his brother, or having quite different, but in their own eyes, moral views.

15. *The Dark Night of Resistance*, pp. xviii–xix.

16. Ibid., p. xxiii.

17. *No Bars to Manhood*, p. 49.

18. Ibid., p. 34.

19. Ibid., p. 36.

20. *The Geography of Faith*, p. 125.

21. Coles asks Berrigan if he has been talking to "a wide range of people." Daniel answers: "Right: with people who have been in jail as conscientious objectors, with people who are weighing their future course of action as political activists, with communications people, with artists and poets and teachers." These would represent a quite narrow range of people—within one segment of the new class. See Coles, op. cit., p. 38.

22. Ibid., pp. 117–18. Other quotes in this and the preceding paragraph will be found here and on pp. 115 and 128.

23. "Believe me, the burning of draft files by men and women like us is a kind of preliminary and particular judgment. It has to do with the end of a long patience." *No Bars to Manhood*, p. 41.

24. Coles, op. cit., p. 170. Appeals to manhood abound in *No Bars to Manhood*, as on pp. 143–44.

25. Ibid., p. 172.

26. Ibid., chapter 3, "At the Edge."

27. "Harrisburg: The Politics of Salvation," *The New York Review of Books* June 15, 1972, p. 36.

28. Coles, op. cit., p. 36.

29. Ibid.

30. *No Bars to Manhood*, p. 62.

31. Coles, op. cit., p. 116.

32. Ibid., p. 81.

33. *No Bars to Manhood*, p. 73.

34. Coles, op. cit., p. 82.

35. Ibid., p. 86. Emphasis supplied.

36. Ibid., p. 48.

37. Quoted by Francine Gray, *The New York Review of Books*, June 1, 1972, pp. 20–21.

There is in today's campus turbulence a new style in conspiracy—conspiracy that is extremely subtle and devious and hence difficult to understand. It is a conspiracy reflected by questionable moods and attitudes, by unrestrained individualism, by nonconformism in dress and speech, even obscene language, rather than by formal membership in specific organizations. Often called the New Left, this conspiracy has unloosed disrespect for the law, contempt for our institutions of free government, and disdain for spiritual and moral values.

—J. Edgar Hoover

The FBI faced the necessity of smashing the legitimacy, the effectiveness, even the sense of internal community of the "action movement"—if it was to do its job in the overall political economy of the empire.

—Arthur Waskow

American Capitalism and American Catholicism: On Collision Course?

ARTHUR I. WASKOW

ONE WAY TO UNDERSTAND the Harrisburg trial is as the audible crash of a remarkable collision: a collision between the FBI and one wing of the Catholic church in America. In the long run, what is important is whether that collision grows into an even greater one, between the great body of American Catholics and the central institutions and practices of American capitalism. But even now, we must try to understand why the political police of the American empire at home should have collided with so strange a band of "criminals": priests, nuns, committedly Catholic lay people—and one odd Pakistani. *Catholic radicals:* how did there even come into being a phrase so strange to American ears, how did there come to be such people? And why did the FBI care?

First, let us look at the Catholic side of the collision. Ten scant years before the indictments—in 1961—one could hardly have imagined Catholic radicals in America. Cardinal Spellman seemed to embody American Catholicism. Pope John XXIII had forced open the windows of the Church a crack, but *Pacem in Terris* was still undreamed of. The last symbolic barrier to Catholic assimilation into America had been broken: the first Catholic president had just been inaugurated. Priests and nuns had not yet been arrested in civil-rights demonstrations.

Arthur Waskow is a fellow at the Institute for Policy Studies in Washington. He has written extensively on the New Left and on new experiments in Judaism. He has authored *The Bush is Burning* and *Freedom Seder: A New Haggadah for Passover.*

Why then, by 1971, had dozens of Catholic clergy and laity taken part in actions to burn U.S. government files, destroy corporate computer memories, and otherwise sabotage the military-industrial complex? The answer cannot be sought alone from the social and political upheavals in American society during the sixties; for some of those upheavals themselves, and in particular the Catholic insurgency, have far deeper roots: roots that predate the existence of the United States.

Indeed, the Catholic insurgency was not merely Catholic by accident: it was perhaps the strongest case of a general religious upheaval that was affecting many of the country's young people. And by *religious* I mean concerned with the most profound questions of what it means for human beings to be alive in the universe. Some people hesitate, are embarrassed, to call their feelings about these issues religious; and they might just as easily be called philosophical, or existential, or spiritual, or even cultural—rather than religious. But what is important is that a profound reexamination of the relation of mankind and the universe was undertaken by many people: a reexamination not only in thought but in action and life-process. For some this upheaval meant the search for ecstasy, with or without drugs; for some, the search for community and the creation of communes, with or without an explicit religious form; for some, a probing of Buddhism, Tao, the *I Ching*, yoga, astrology; for some, a probing into the roots of Judaism, Christianity, Islam, and an attempt to reawaken them; for some, the reexamination and remaking of Marxism with a new attention to spiritual and cultural revolution.

One group of these upheavals, the group most directly relevant to the emergence of Catholic radicalism, comes ultimately from an event, a process that began 3,500 years ago. For the Catholics emerge from a tradition that harks back to the moment when Moses stood in the wilderness of Midian and, out of his memories of death and despair in Egypt, was challenged; challenged by a bush that burned and burned yet was not consumed, challenged to become the liberator of his people. And, in return, challenged the Voice from the bush to give his name. And in response heard

the new name of an old God: I am Becoming Who I am
Becoming. A moment of consummate power, political, theological, existential.

It is easy for those who take that moment seriously to believe
that they stand today at the same kind of place and time that
Moses stood. The generation that had its earliest political memories formed by the Nazi holocaust and American Hiroshima
would find it easy to hear again "the cry by reason of oppression"
that ascended from Egypt. The generation of Catholics that had
nightmares of their Church's silence during Auschwitz was also
the generation of Americans that had nightmares of their country's celebration of Hiroshima. The fiery nightmares of Auschwitz
and Hiroshima were confirmed in napalm in Vietnam. Such a
generation, schooled in burning, would find it easy to see the
human race itself as our generation's bush that burns and burns,
yet is not consumed. Indeed, the whole human race—not only
part. For this generation is the first in which the danger is total
and the cry of despair grows from the fear of the impending
death of all mankind.

Could such a prospect fail to affect those who trace their
traditions to the bush? For the God who spoke there connected
his very being and becoming to the liberation of human beings in
slavery. The God of Sinai defined himself at the beginning of the
Ten Commandments not as the creator of heaven and earth, nor
as the giver of grace to souls, but as the liberator from Egypt. The
death of all mankind would surely mean the death of such a
God.

What is more, those who trace their traditions to the bush
remember that the Voice recognized his own inadequacies under
his old "names"—that is, according to the ways he had hitherto
been understood. For the traditional understandings of the God of
Abraham had been insufficient to help the Jews liberate themselves from Pharaoh. Who could miss the knowledge that in the
generation of the H-bomb, the old ideas of God had become
inadequate to human liberation and human survival? Somehow
the names by which even the Church had known God were

inadequate to keep even the Church from worshiping idols; and the same tradition said very clearly what the cost of idolatry is: the idols have eyes that do not see, ears that cannot hear, hands that do not feel; they are dead, and those who make them become, like them, dead. In our day that is all too literally true: those who make and worship the idols of the state, wealth, power, technology are all too clearly doomed to die.

On the other hand, the tradition gave a promise too: to choose life is to bring the messianic age. The human race which can now for the first time in its history make the deliberate choice of universal death can also make the choice of universal liberation. The knowledge which makes possible the one can make possible the other. That is: the end of war and exploitation; the reunion of men and women with their work and with the natural universe.

In the deepest sense, therefore, the collision of radical Catholics and the FBI begins with the rediscovery of the seeds of Catholicism. The same process had begun among other religious communities that remember the same events—among Jews and among the new Black converts to a new version of Islam. But these are indeed traditions, not a single tradition, and the responses have not have identical. There may be a sense in which both the Catholic and Muslim responses have been a little more Jewish than the norm of their traditions—for instance, more oriented to the Exodus specifically. (For example, see Daniel Berrigan's fascination with Passover in *The Dark Night of the Resistance* and Elijah Muhammad's apocalypse of the plagues that will destroy Pharaonic America while liberating the Black nation.) Such a Jewish overtone would not be surprising in a situation where serious Christians and Muslims found themselves in the kind of minority underground status that they have not known for more than a millennium but which Jews have for more than that millennium known, and learned to suffer and to cope with.

Still, even if it is correct to discern this slight tendency toward a Jewish understanding of the world and a harking back toward the more Jewish memories of Christianity and Islam, there are certain ways in which the Catholic radicals were clearly different from the new kinds of Jews and Muslims. Most important, perhaps, in bringing them into collision with the FBI was their deep incorporation of the Christian tradition of martyrdom. Jews and Moslems have also had martyrs, of course, and they have been honored; but to take one very rough index, the "maximum heroes" of the three traditions had different reactions to martyrdom. Both Moses and Mohammed fled their homes to avoid it; Jesus accepted it willingly, almost triumphantly. The Jewish norm continues to be the building of community and the practice of the Paths, to the point of martyrdom only if absolutely necessary. The norm of Islam continues to be the building of community until the day when infidels and oppressors can be destroyed. It was easier for Catholics than it would have been for Jews or Muslims to burn draft-board files and then stand celebrating until the police arrived. And that brought the Catholic radicals into direct collision with the FBI.

If we look now at the FBI's side of the collision, we have of course a much shorter tradition to examine. But there is a tradition. The FBI was born in 1908, during the period of great growth in the Socialist party of Gene Debs, the period of Wobbly triumphs. In the beginning there was vigorous criticism. But after 1918–20, when J. Edgar Hoover consolidated his power in and over the bureau, criticism became marginal. Then, during 1970–71, something went out of kilter. Suddenly serious presidential candidates and congressional leaders began criticizing the bureau. Worse, somebody or somebodies actually made it look ridiculous by liberating a set of its files from its office in Media, Pennsylvania, and in the process proved the extent of its repressiveness. And while the establishment press did not quite applaud these unknown open-information zealots, it didn't let slip the dogs of war against them either. For the first time in fifty years, the sacrosanct bureau was in political trouble.

But how had Hoover and the bureau become sacrosanct in the first place? In the 1918–20 period, Hoover headed the General Information Division—the political section. He was busy, in

those days calling race riots the product of Black bolsheviks.
Jailing draft resisters. Raiding hundreds of radicals' homes and
offices without warrants. Deporting thousands of radicals. Breaking the Wobblies. Breaking the Socialist party. Breaking, indeed,
the last great radical movement of Americans that actually threatened the system.

The triumph of the FBI in those days was not accomplished
solely by repression. It never is. Radical movements do not grow
or die according to whether the government tries to smash them.
Governments always try, but some radical movements grow anyway. Repression only works if the government is also trying to
meet most of the human needs of its people, or seems to be
trying.

And that points to why for the first time in fifty years the FBI
was having serious trouble. The country's mood toward the FBI is
a kind of index of the country's mood toward the whole of
American capitalism. And by 1970 that index had remarkably
declined. Not since 1920, not even in the worst moments of the
Great Depression, had so many Americans doubted that the
government was even trying to meet human needs. American
capitalism was in one of its periodic crises, and this time it was
not easy to see what the way out could be. In 1920 the way out
was a consumer prosperity that led stright to the Great Depression. In 1940 the way out was a decision to spend hundreds of
billions of dollars of public funds—not for the poor or for schools
or hospitals or housing, but for war. Spending on civilian needs
at the level we spent on World War II and the Cold War would
have dislocated the American class structure—would have moved
up the lowest rungs of the class ladder so drastically that the
nature of the ladder itself might have come into question. But
Franklin Roosevelt and those who with him ruled America were
not prepared to endanger the ladder. So all through the Great
Depression, only piddling funds were spent on civilian needs.

But when foreign-policy problems arose, it turned out to be
fairly easy to spend on the military. Spending public funds for
war did not seem to benefit any one class, any one rung on the

ladder. It looked like money spent on the flag, on the nation. And in fact, it ended up benefiting the great corporations more than anyone else; it strengthened the ladder rather than endangering it. So in 1940 those who ruled the nation dealt with the internal crisis of American capitalism by creating the first large, permanent war machine in American history. (I am talking about results, not intentions. I am not saying that the sole, or chief, or even necessarily a major reason for creating the war machine was to deal with the economic crisis. There were certainly major foreign-policy reasons. But it *was* the war machine, not TVA or AAA or NLRA or HOLC, which ended mass unemployment.)

That answer kept American capitalism working into the mid-sixties. The new war machine defeated Germany and Japan, established American power in the heart of Europe and the coast of Asia. And at home it kept production and employment high, meeting the private sector's chronic deficit in creating both. But in the sixties both the foreign and domestic justifications for the war machine began to weaken. A war machine that was based on the threat of destroying the human race several times over began to look dangerous, even to Americans. A war machine that couldn't defeat a crowd of peasant gooks began to look silly. And at home, people started noticing that even basic civilian needs— schools, hospitals, sewers, houses—weren't being met. People started connecting the constant price inflation with a full generation of spending 10 percent of the gross national product on the military, thus giving workers who needed things to eat, wear or live in, solid wages for producing—what? Weapons. Things that nobody could eat, wear, or live in. People then competed to buy a constricted supply of the food, clothes, and housing that they needed. They started noticing that the government was trying to control inflation by increasing unemployment. And slowly, as the sixties ended, middle Americans began to get angry. The crisis of American capitalism which had affected chiefly marginal Americans—Blacks, students, Chicanos—through the sixties began to reach factory workers, secretaries, shopkeepers, civil servants, insurance salesmen. And as 1970 began, wildcat strikes multiplied; the first massive strike ever by federal employees, an illegal postal strike, was attempted and was successful; protests against inflation and unemployment rose; fury at rotten schools, health care, housing began to boil over.

Now what has all this thumbnail history to do with the FBI and a bunch of radical Catholics? Just this: great chunks of that Middle America which was in 1970–71 barely beginning to get angry is Catholic. The great immigrant communities of the late nineteenth and early twentieth centuries—Poles and Italians, especially, and even still the Irish of a generation earlier—were being squeezed to the wall by the effects of the war machine. Indeed, they had been among the dispossessed of America since they arrived. For despite the victories of the political machines they voted for, they received few of the benefits created by their work and their votes: the cream was skimmed by the bosses of the machines. But the Catholic church has rarely in the past encouraged them to rebel against the corporations and the bosses, and since 1945 it had been one of the strongest supporters of the war machine as a way of dealing with Communism. Indeed, for generations the Church has been one of the absolutely crucial engines for pacifying Middle America. Controlling insurgency. Linking, through the ideology of private property, the auto worker who goes not quite head-over-heels in debt to buy a barely adequate house to the bank that lends him the money at high interest. Reinforcing in its schools and its confessionals the Puritan ethic—far more correctly the establishment Catholic ethic—of hard work, little joy, and anger at those who dare to play. Blessing every soldier who fought or prepared to fight the holy war against the godless Communist world conspiracy. Schooling indeed the very men who staffed the FBI.

But something happened. During the sixties, the Church in America grew a left wing: some might say miraculously, but the FBI knew it was a demonic miracle. There emerged Catholics whom some called libertarians—but the FBI knew them as libertines. Catholic pacifists—whom the FBI knew were subversives. Catholics who joined Black sit-ins and Chicano picket lines. And that posed a danger to the empire that was really deadly. For if Catholic priests, nuns, already one crazy old Pope—God knows, perhaps next some archbishops!—were to break with American capitalism, stop integrating Catholic workers into the personality structures, political assumptions, and careers that kept American capitalism going, . . . if they linked up with the reviving anger of Catholic workers being buffeted by the most recent crisis of American capitalism . . .

Then there might be an earthquake.

And this the FBI could not permit. Out of some primordial sense, perhaps some memory of the era of its birth, it smelled the new crisis of capitalism. It sniffed out those who might help transform that crisis into an earthquake. It said to the Catholic church, essentially: "You are *forbidden* to stop being what you have been. You are *forbidden* to define being Catholic as a mission of rebellion instead of pacification. You are *forbidden* to disturb, shake, question what has been one of our most useful instruments of social control."

So Harrisburg. So the hounding not only of a Jesuit and a Josephite, but also of a woman who had been president of two leading Catholic upper-class women's colleges. Not *despite* the fact that Jogues Egan was who she was, but *because* of it.

Again, I am talking of results more than intentions. I do not know whether J. Edgar Hoover was wholly conscious of his role in the American Empire, and was wholly conscious of the deep threat that radical Catholics posed. He may well have used those more primitive senses, taste and smell, rather than a level open-eyed gaze when he singled out the Catholic movement for special treatment. It does not much matter. For the Catholics were dangerous, and the FBI *did* recognize that. Thus Harrisburg.

The precipitating factor that brought the head-on collision between Catholics newly facing what they saw as the burning bush and an FBI grimly determined to protect American capitalism was, of course, the Vietnam War. More specifically, it was a new and deeper crisis in that war.

In early 1970, when the Harrisburg indictments were drawn,

that war was going badly: the peoples of an agrarian, poverty-stricken, weaponless, powerless peninsula had banded together to stalemate, sometimes to defeat, the most powerful, wealthy, high-technologied empire in human history. The empire tried to respond by escalating the war, but at home a spirited movement had made that very hard. In six years' time, from the teach-in spring of 1965 to the Mayday spring of 1971, the American people had turned around. Those Americans who explained, demonstrated, resisted, helped create the fact that 73 percent of the American people wanted all the troops home by the end of the year. Most of the time, most of the people of any empire applaud the military power that keeps the empire expanding. But not this time.

Still, the empire was not ready to give up. Instead it faced the final crisis of the war by playing one last trump card: trying to computerize the war. The new approach was billed as "Vietnam-ization," but in fact the Vietnamese were no readier to fight for the Saigon government than they ever had been. Machines, however, were ready to fight: the "electronic battlefield" and massive bombing of huge areas of South Vietnam, Laos, and Cambodia replaced foot soldiers. If Indochina could not be conquered, it could at least be destroyed. Bring the troops home but destroy Indochina from the air. Who, said the government, will object to that?

Certainly the Catholic radicals would. And they had become the leading edge of the antiwar movement: those who were inflict-ing the greatest political, moral, and even—since they did non-violent sabotage—the greatest material damage on the empire. The Catholic radicals pushed out the limits of thinkable antiwar activity without endangering human life. In so doing, they gave even moderate antiwar feeling new space in which to express itself politically and new alarming reasons that it *should* express itself politically: that is, the fear of turmoil if the war did not end quickly. What the draft resistance had earlier undertaken in opposing the ground war, the Catholic saboteurs would certainly continue in '71 if the government computerized the war: direct interference with the war, violation of normal law, in order to point the way to millions of moderate and liberals who otherwise might relax when the troops come back.

So in 1971 the Catholic radicals posed the greatest political danger to the carrying out of a central policy of the imperial government. In such circumstances, classically, an empire turns for help to its political police. Meanwhile, the political police themselves are often so anxious to bring their own expertise to bear that they may even be slightly ahead of the empire. And so, in 1970–71 the predilections of the FBI and of the Mitchell-Kleindienst imperial policy group meshed. The FBI faced the necessity of smashing the legitimacy, the effectiveness, even the sense of internal community of the "action movement"—if it was to do its job in the overall political economy of the empire. How to do this?

Here was the FBI's recipe: Has the movement built a strong sense of community within the ranks? Then shatter the trust on which such a community must rest by infiltrating informers into it, and then make that trust harder to achieve among other would-be insurgent communities in the future by surfacing the informer and making it clear that other communities will be infiltrated. Has the movement won moral support precisely because it has destroyed wicked property without endangering human life? Then the political police must assert that the Catholic radicals *have* endangered human life by planning to blow up heating plants and kidnap officials. Did a remarkable number of American respond to the first accusations with skepticism and disillusionment about the FBI? Then back the accusations up by escalating, just as successive waves of disillusionment with the war have been answered with successive escalations. For example, use contempt citations to widen the war to include their comrades too.

The goal was simple: break the action movement, and blunt the whole antiwar movement, before it could mobilize massive opposition to the empire's computerization of the war, or link up with the uneasiness of working-class Catholics. And do it quickly.

WHO WON?

At Harrisburg the FBI won. Not legally, but politically. The FBI's victory was achieved at two political levels: the level of the antiwar movement and the level of basic political change in the United States, but not at the level of spiritual and religious transformation.

First of all, the antiwar movement was, for at least eighteen months, deprived of the effective leadership and daring of the Catholic radicals. It is impossible to prove whether American responses to the war would have been any different during the period from January 1971 to June 1972 if the Catholic radicals had not been immoblized by the Harrisburg trial, but it can be argued that their absence badly weakened the radical wing of the antiwar movement, and that the weakness of the antiwar radicals then considerably weakened the effectiveness of antiwar action as a whole. Let us compare the history of this period to that of two earlier crises of the war: the one in 1967–68 and the one in early 1970. In 1967–68, the draft resistance movement, street actions at the Pentagon, on campuses, and at induction centers, and in some ways the Black urban uprisings, were the cutting edge of the antiwar movement, and helped make space for the more moderate McCarthy and Robert Kennedy presidential campaigns. Together, according to the Pentagon papers, the radical and liberal antiwar tactics put limits on the options that the Johnson administration felt it could use in responding to the Tet uprising. Again, in 1970, the tempestuous nationwide campus strike after the Cambodia invasion helped spark legislative and liberal oppositon to the war; the Nixon administration retreated—temporarily—from its readiness to escalate the war; and Congess forbade interventions in Cambodia and Laos.

In 1971–72, things were different. Not that the war was winding down: simply that the antiwar movement did not have the energy to puncture that myth, in the way it had punctured so many previous Johnson and Nixon administration myths of seeking peace. Indeed these eighteen months were the period of the greatest itensification of the U.S. air war against South Vietnam; the refusal of the Nixon administration to use the opportunity of the South Vietnamese elections to drop its support of the Thieu government and move toward a coalition in Saigon; its decision instead to seek once more a military victory in the South; the resulting spring offensive of 1972 by the NLF and North Vietnamese; and the Nixon administration's response in escalation of the war through the bombing of North Vietnam's cities, the mining of its ports, and the blockade of its coasts. It was also the first period since 1965 when leadership of the antiwar movement was exercised not by radicals using teach-ins, draft resistance, mass rallies, street marches, sit-downs, campus strikes, and similarly militant tactics; but instead by liberals using legislative and electoral tactics. Yet these tactics by themselves proved ineffective. Laws that tried to push the administration into setting a date for the end of U.S. military action in Vietnam and that tried to prohibit the use of American arms or American-paid mercenaries in Cambodia or Laos were simply ignored by the administration after Congress had passed them.

What if during those eighteen months the antiwar movement had included a growing tax-refusal campaign, nonviolent sabotage of munitions plants and airfields, sit-downs on military highways and at military ports? It is impossible to be sure, but easy to imagine that the administration would have had a much harder time.

Was the Harrisburg trial crucial to the sapping of radical antiwar energies? Again, it is impossible to be sure; but Harrisburg did not stand alone.

First, the radical antiwar movement was confronted at almost the same moment with the unconstitutional sweep arrests on Mayday in Washington of thousands of young people not charged with illegal behavior; the sudden widespread use of grand juries and contempt citations to fish for information and turn untalkative radicals into instant criminals; the charging of a noted Black radical—since proved innocent—with terrorism and murder; and even an unprecedented attempt at prior censorship of the country's leading newspapers. Some radicals quailed, and others simply found their hands full (and their pockets empty) dealing with the wave of legal attacks. So Harrisburg seems to have been at least one element in the decline of radical action against the war.

Second, the FBI won a limited and probably temporary victory at Harrisburg over the creation of a more basic opposition to American capitalism. Most obviously, indictments and trial helped squelch some stirrings of interest among the Catholic activists in the possibility of connecting their own radical analysis with deepening anger and malaise in the Catholic working class. Late in 1970, the radical Catholics had been debating next directions: continued draft-board or other antiwar actions? anticorporate actions like attacks on Dow Chemical Company? proworker actions like the liberation and free distribution of food from supermarkets in working-class neighborhoods where inflation was taking meat and other foods off the table? These discussions were aborted, as it suddenly seemed necessary to focus entirely on defense against the Harrisburg indictments and the related legal harassment.

But there were less obvious ways in which the FBI made harder the creation of an alternative to American capitalism. The publicly celebrated use of informers, infiltrators, surveillants, and *agents provocateur* was bound to have a corrosive effect on the creation of alternative communities working on the principle and practice of trust and love, rather than profit and hierarchy. Not only "underground" communities like those of the radical Catholic saboteurs were corroded by the Harrisburg disclosures, but even dissident but "legal" communities working together on projects like communal farms, free schools, food co-ops, neighborhood health clinics, found themselves after Harrisburg doubting the reality of their community, the practicality of their openness, the possibility of trust. In the FBI files published from Media, Pennsylvania, one memo had encouraged FBI agents to let the public know bits and pieces of their pervasive surveillance precisely in order to encourage paranoia in the antiwar movement. Harrisburg was a gigantic world-wide acting out of that memo. It weakened the "associational" ability of Americans that Tocqueville was so fond of and impressed by—an associational ability which he found as the key factor making democracy possible in America. The damaging of the very ability to associate was therefore damaging not only of individual civil liberties—which is how the use of informers and surveillants is usually viewed in American law—but of the very fabric of American democracy. Many of the new communities which felt most keenly the effects of Harrisburg had themselves been formed precisely *because* their members had felt associational democracy and their own citizenly identities to be in retreat before huge bureaucratic and capitalist organizational systems. The FBI intrusions were thus a kind of second-level attack: when bureaucratic and market pressures had failed to break the spirit of community, had perhaps even caused it to be reborn, police power was brought in to break it up. The obvious question is whether the new communities are so fragile as to have no way of resisting this police pressure—short of destroying from within their own sense of community and participation. The question must wait to be answered by more history.

Finally, the FBI won a victory at Harrisburg simply by daring to charge Catholic priests with violence and conspiracy. It did not matter that the prosecution lost; it had opened up new space to the right by doing what would have been outrageous a year before. In 1971 the whole domestic effort of the government was to open up rightward space in this way: censor the New York *Times*, sweep innocent people off the streets in dragnet arrests, etc. No matter that the *Times* finally got the right to publish the Pentagon papers; no matter that the Mayday young people were freed by the courts; no matter that the Harrisburg defendants were acquitted of conspiracy. The unthinkable had been made doable.

This was, of course, precisely the mirror image of the intention of the political tactics of the radical Catholics themselves: they did not expect their actions to "win" in the most immediate sense—

for example, to stop the draft by burning records; but they did expect to open up new leftward space for antiwar action. What was at first blush surprising was to find the use of "extremist" politics in the White House and the Justice Department. But within the Nixon administration during 1970–71 there was growing in power a nonestablishment southwestern coalition of the nouveaux riches and nouveaux puissants, a coalition holding extremist tactical tendencies. Together with the military and the increasingly right-wing police forces, it showed signs of seeking to become an alternative to the traditional eastern establishment as a base for governing the United States. For the first time in history a spokesman for Texas oil rather than eastern banking had been made secretary of the treasury. The secretary of defense was a right-wing Wisconsin congressman, not a great industrial executive. The secretary of state had Wall Street ties, but was being ignored by the president. The attorney general was a Wall Street lawyer, but from a minor firm, and in mid-1971 he felt perfectly comfortable in trying to establish prior censorship over the eastern establishment's prime newspaper, the *New York Times*. All this indicated the existence of a political base within the administration that explains its readiness to use the extremist tactics of pressing a political campaign not in order to win but in order to open up new space on the right.

In these ways the FBI and its allies within the Nixon administration weakened the new radical energies that were beginning to propose and create an alternative to American capitalism. But they were not able to weaken the most potent energy that underlay the radical political groups: the energies of religious and spiritual transformation. Those energies came from Americans who were conscious that they had had set before them the choice of life and death, and were choosing life that they and their children might live—conscious of the choice as a religious one, choosing life in the most profound sense, and seeing American capitalism as having become hooked on death. Even as the radical Catholics came under legal pressures, they themselves created new political-liturgical forms; and the new Quaker, Episcopal, Mennonite, Jewish, Buddhist, and yogic communities continued to grow, to examine questions of the polity and ecology as a whole, a "system" to be religiously questioned and confronted.

Yet the religious-political upheaval that has been taking place in many parts of American society cannot, on its own showing so far, transform the society. The major question that emerges from Harrisburg is, therefore, whether the collision between the FBI and the radical Catholics is an incident or a portent. Will millions of Americans be able to make clear to themselves the ultimacy, the profundity, the basic nature of the universequake that is upon us; accept that it is a religious transformation they are facing; and create the liturgies, the communities, the new names of God that will free them to live? Will the seriously religious elements of the Catholic church decide to address the life-and-death problems of the Catholic working class as vigorously and profoundly as many of them have addressed the problem of the Vietnam War, and if so how will they be able to link their own energies directly to those of workers? Will Americans other than the radical Catholics be able to bring the new religious consciousness to bear on the Vietnam War itself, in such a way as to resist and interfere with it rather than simply denounce it?

The present seeming quiescence of insurgency is no answer to these questions. For that quiescence may be a sign of death or of the quiet spreading of seeds from a dead plant into new earth. The FBI's tactical success at Harrisburg may have contributed to the death of this generation's radical movement or may simply have forced it to seed itself more widely and deeply in the society.

A plain lack of political direction and political substance makes the politics of the Berrigans seem apolitical. It seems like a politics of resentment, anger, desperation—but not a politics going any place in particular, creating a constituency, fulfilling a larger program.

—Michael Novak

I really have to hand it to that Father Berrigan, he showed them (he showed me and a lot of people watching) that he wasn't going to sit back and be shoved around by those guys, just because they did him the biggest favor this side of Heaven—let him be on their show.

—Boston factory worker after watching an interview of Father Daniel Berrigan on *Meet the Press*

Ordinary Hopes, Ordinary Fears

ROBERT COLES

THE AMERICAN PEOPLE I have worked with in recent years have by and large remained indifferent to the social and political message of the Berrigans, among other radical critics of our society; many of the families I have visited have not even heard of Daniel or Philip Berrigan, or if they have heard their names, somehow ears have refused access to words, acts and, yes, even prolonged events, like the Harrisburg trial.

I had best right off let a factory worker speak; he is from a town north of Boston, is Catholic, is thirty, has a wife and four children, graduated from high school, takes the Boston *Globe,* a liberal paper which has given a great deal of attention to the Berrigans: "Well, maybe I *have* heard about them; I know there are some priests who are giving the Church a hard time. I guess there's more protest in this country than before. I haven't got the time for any of that—my mind has other worries. Let the priests shout, and the colored, and the students. I work. I'm up at five o'clock and out of the house in fifteen minutes. I don't even make myself a cup of coffee, because I don't want to disturb the wife. I'm at work by six, and I don't see my family until seven at night. I've got two jobs, not just one. I leave one and go to the other. How's that for keeping on the go? When I come home I want to sit and have a good supper, and talk with my wife and children, and maybe watch television for an hour—but I'll tell you, it puts

---

Robert Coles has written extensively on middle Americans, youth, the drug culture and political activists. He co-authored with Daniel Berrigan *The Geography of Faith* and is best known for his three volume study, *Children of Crisis.* Dr. Coles is a psychiatrist with Harvard University.

me to sleep, even a good, funny program does. My wife is always waking me and telling me to pick myself up and get my sleep. Sunday is the only free day I have, and with church and the family to visit—my family and my wife's—it goes fast, that's the one day I see the sun all week. (If there is any sun, and it's not raining and no good out!)

"Who has time to read the papers? That's for my wife, and even she only looks at the ads, and maybe those columns—you know, where they give their free advice. She's got a lot to keep her busy, too. Her mother is sick, and her father, and the children are a handful. I'll hear the news sometimes in my car, and it all goes in one ear and out the next. What's it all about? The politicians, they're out for themselves. They have big egos, that's what. It takes a lot of nerve, to think you can tell others what's right and what's wrong, and make laws for them—for you and me. The college professors, they're the same—a lot of talk, they come up with. I'll tell you something, when I *do* look at the paper, maybe on Sunday, all I care about is the sports page; but if you read the rest of the paper, there's this politician and his promises (they tell more lies than anyone else), and there's another politician and he's contradicting the first guy—and then there's the college professors, giving their free advice, as if any of us care what they have to say. But the papers always pay attention to the professors and those college students, never to us. Let me have something to say, an ordinary working man, and no one's listening—sometimes even my own wife doesn't. But let a kid with long hair and crazy clothes sound off, or his teacher, and the reporters are there, hanging on every word and saying isn't it wonderful, how smart they are and all the new things they have got to tell us. Well, there are a lot of us who have our ideas, only no one bothers to pay attention."

He can speak more bluntly, some would say more crudely, than that; he can lash out with particular bitterness and lack of restraint at people I suppose best characterized, collectively, as upper-middle-class intellectuals, both young and old—men and women who don't have to struggle as he does, and who (so he

cannot stop reminding his listener) have no trouble making
themselves heard. Several times I have tried to point out that
those are not the people who really own or run this country—and
he has willingly picked up on that theme, telling me who is
"really rich" and who "just makes noise." He knows that the
banks, the corporations, "the big money boys" are not to be
confused with "the talkers, the ones who come up with one idea,
then another, while the rest of us work and work and work to keep
the country going."

He even knows how one group (maybe more "silent" than
those called "silent Americans") can escape almost everyone's
attention, while another group becomes all too apparent and
objectionable: "I don't think the college-professor crowd is half
as important as they think they are, or as they'd like to be. They
may write speeches for Senators and Presidents, but they're not
the ones who decide what's going to happen in this country. They
may be on all those television programs, but they don't take in the
profits, not the way Wall Street does. Wall Street is America,
Wall Street and all it stands for. My dad used to tell us that; he
said Roosevelt saved us from Wall Street, greedy, selfish Wall
Street, during the Depression. My dad went to Mass almost every
morning, but for a few years he almost starved to death. He
wouldn't go on relief, though. No, sir. He was too proud. He
would tell me that he used to walk over to the office, the WPA it
was, and then he couldn't get himself to go in. He'd come back
home, and he and my mother and my grandparents and my aunts
and uncles—well, I guess they pooled the little they had and tried
to get by from day to day. Dad told me he was a radical then. He
would go over to the Catholic Worker people. He'd say Jesus
Christ would be against the system we have in this country—with
our cutthroat competition instead of sharing with people. This
country is for the rich, he'd say.

"But things have changed. Where else in the world does the
ordinary working man like myself get a fair break? I mean, we
live a pretty good life here in this country. My great-aunt went
over to Ireland, and she came back and said it's all very well to go

over there on a visit—it's pretty and you really feel close to your roots—but it's no place to live unless you're plenty rich. Here there are the rich, and like the rich everywhere, they're greedy and selfish, I'll keep saying that. But you have a good standard of living here, and your kids, they can work and do even better than you if they want to. There's hope here, and that's important. No one is locked into a place in the society, a place he can't get out of. Well, maybe it's true a lot of the colored are; but a lot of them could be doing better for themselves if they really buckled down and worked, and not take this welfare as if the country owed it to them. There's no question, the poor have it rough; but I still think you can't do better than America. Sometimes I'll see the President on television, and I'll say that's a lot of two-bit, phony talk he's coming up with. 'Do you believe him?' my wife will say, and I'll answer *no*, I sure don't. He takes his cues from Wall Street, I can hear my dad's voice in my own voice! But my dad said before he died that he was glad he'd lived long enough to see us all own our homes, each of his sons, and that's more than he ever could do. So, you have to take the bad with the good, like my wife will tell the children. They'll ask her why we have these wars, and why some people have everything and a lot of people don't have much of anything (they hear these things in church, in school and on television), and what can you say to them but it's always been like that, since the beginning of the world, and maybe one day it'll change, maybe one day we'll have honest men running the government and we'll all share and share alike, but let me tell you, I don't expect to see it, that day—you'd have to have people think different (be less for themselves) and you'd have to have a new kind of system, where there wouldn't be the stock market, I guess, and everything would belong to the working people of the country. But who can figure all that kind of thing out? I've got enough to do keeping up with the food prices—I'm barely with my head above water now!"

I can't believe that the inconsistencies and ambiguities which come across in that particular man's words (pulled together from much longer and necessarily less pointed, more rambling conver-

sations we have had these recent years) ought strike anyone as all
that surprising—and yet I am not sure many of us who write or
read essays such as this have taken great pain to understand, not
only what such a factory worker thinks and feels, but, perhaps
more to the point, what prophetic social and religious critics like
the Berrigans "mean" or "do" (yes, psychologically and spiritu-
ally) to a man who once in a tired and frustrated and bitterly
radical mood said to me: "I came back from church today and I
heard the priest talk about Jesus Christ our Lord and the money-
changers. He got so mad at them, that He went after them; He
probably didn't hit them, because He was too kind for that, but
He tried to drive them out of the temple. I'd like to drive out
some of the fat cats in this country—the people who gouge you,
push the prices higher, eat their big, fat, tax-deductible lunches,
while I'm going, all the time going, just to be able to stay out of
the clutches of Household Finance and their sweet, come-dance-
with-me invitations that forget to mention how much interest
you'll end up paying. There must be a better way to run a country— we have a few rich and lots of people barely getting by, and
then we have the welfare chiselers. This country is too rich for
anyone to go broke, like my brother did, because his wife fell sick
and then came the doctor's bills and the hospital bills, and they
just wiped him out."

Every once in a while I have had no trouble figuring out what
he believes. I have in mind one Sunday when a parish priest was
not the one speaking, though the words in many respects were
comparable to Christ's in their emphasis on social justice and
scorn for the powerful, the first who shall, alas, only in a far-off
day become the last. Then, contrary to what I have just quoted
him saying, there was time for more than a few of those moments
of television that precede sleep, the kind of "dead sleep" he has
told me he experiences. I sat with him on a Sunday, and we both
watched Daniel Berrigan appear on *Meet the Press*—he had just
been released from Danbury prison, and the Harrisburg trial was
very much in the offing. Neither of us spoke during the entire half
hour Father Berrigan was interviewed, though toward the end I

heard a loud "he's right"—and to be candid, I have to admit I was convinced that I was sure the remark was directed at one of the reporters rather than their Jesuit "subject." Afterwards I asked "who was right" and was promptly told "the father." I explained that I must have missed the point—and I was not being disingenuous, though condescending, perhaps that. He told me what "the point" was; he explained to me in blunt and emotional words what reporters can do to the spirit of a man, to his intentions and efforts (and maybe social scientists like me ought to wonder more often whether the words to follow don't apply to *us* as well): "The father was trying to say how he feels about injustice all over the world, and those smart-aleck reporters were trying to corner him with their clever questions. They looked like a bunch of stuffed shirts to me, wise-guy stuffed shirts who like to embarrass people but have never done a single good deed in their whole lives. Jesus Christ could come before them, or one of the apostles, and they'd be sitting there with their big-shot looks on their faces, trying to figure out what *His* angle is. The father got fed up with them, and he told them so—not by what he said, but you could just see it on his face. It's too bad more people don't do that.

"I watch programs like *Meet the Press* sometimes, and turn them off, because it's hard to know who is worse, the reporters with their know-it-all looks and questions or the politicians, always trying to win a few million more votes with some opinion that I can hear meaning one thing and my wife or my next door neighbor can hear meaning something else. I really have to hand it to that Father Berrigan, he showed them (he showed me and a lot of people watching) that he wasn't going to sit back and be shoved around by those guys, just because they did him the biggest favor this side of Heaven—let him be on their show."

So, Father Berrigan had been "right" when he lost a little of his "cool"; and meanwhile I had to live with my own particular reaction to the same stimulus—I had concluded rather quickly that Father Berrigan had been "wrong," had displayed unwisely his impatience, had committed a "tactical blunder," had dis-

played a touch of the "arrogance" some of his critics had for a
long time charged him with. (Sometimes I wonder what the
critics of the Berrigans would do if they didn't have that word
"arrogance" to summon every time the concrete witness of those
two brothers and their friends challenges us.)

Perhaps I have no right to ask that such an incident sustain
any large-scale argument of mine. Still, I wonder how unusual or
idiosyncratic that encounter of sorts was—between a nervous
intellectual, worried what "they" might think and conclude, and
one of "them," who ought to have long ago proved to me he was
no fool. Yet, each time he has done so, has proved that, I have not
quite believed him, or believed him only for so long or so far. Not
that there is only one side to this or other working men and
women I have heard and tried to learn from, the first long series
of remarks shows rather clearly how angry, bitter, scornful and
spiteful he can become—turning confusion into rage, frustration
into hate, a moment's radical impulse into a prolonged, chauvin-
istic defense of the status quo.

I have heard from him words, phrases, long and angry sentences that I would not want set down here—and I hasten to add
that there might well be a few moments and more in the life of us
proudly self-aware and educated, confidently "liberal" or "radical" social critics or observers which we might not, in retrospect,
wish to have recorded and placed before the eyes of others.
Nevertheless, he is not uncommonly able to reverse himself, shift
gears with a decisiveness and abruptness that apparently I have
not sufficiently come to take for granted—or fit into my mind's
way of looking at him. Hence the constant surprises I seem to
experience as he comes forth with one or another statement, all of
them spoken in a living room it is rather too easy for the likes of
me to stereotype as thoroughly and unfairly as he can do with
respect to people or locations I happen to like or feel close to.
And does not the man himself help me along, as I summon my
stereotypes, when he indicates how grateful he is for what this
country has given him—the house; the attached garage with its
two cars, one new and one not so new, but not old, either; the

television sets, the washing machine and drying machine and electric stove and refrigerator with its nearby companion—that freezer stuffed to the brim with colorfully packaged foods?

The point is not the *presence* of ambiguity, but the capacity in any number of us for sudden and even outspoken shifts of opinion. Why do they take place—under what circumstances? Was it Daniel Berrigan's "arrogance" which won over in a flash that somewhat stolid Catholic factory worker—who in 1968 voted for Nixon out of disgust at the hippies and yippies and God knows what other groups who seemed to him so tied to the democratic party—*his* party, he used to think? Did he, rather, identify with the weaker man in an argument, feel himself, like Daniel Berrigan, the aggrieved man always pushed around by powerful and all too self-assured interests, parties, groups?

I did not ask him those questions, of course. Anyway, once aroused, he needed no prodding from me; he was quite willing to make his reasons (his complicated range of affiliations and loyalties, doubts and suspicions) rather clear: "The man is a priest. I may disagree with him, but he's given his life over to God; he's no two-bit politician trying to work his way up some ladder, and he's no holier-than-thou professor, in love with his own words, or snotty overgrown kid, living off his parents and preaching to the rest of us who keep the country going—turning out the food and the cars and the machines, the little things, too, that he takes for granted. He's a priest, and listening to him, you can feel he's honest, he's a decent man. He may be wrong, as a lot of priests are, because they're too idealistic, that's why. But when those reporters turned on him with their clever little questions, I suddenly thought to myself: just look at them and listen to them, with their fancy suits and hair slicked down and talking big and fancy, with potatoes in their mouths, as if they've been to England to polish themselves up, and being so full of themselves, and quizzing him as though they were half district attorney, half bishop or cardinal, and meanwhile he's trying to be nice to them, but they keep egging him on, and finally he's had enough and he let's them know it, but he kept up his dignity, he didn't blow up or get sarcastic, the way they do every Sunday. He just gave them a look and got silent on them. I'm with a priest like him every-time against those people, even if I don't go along with all he's saying. I was for Bobby Kennedy, even if I didn't go along with him on everything, either."

Bobby Kennedy—the man who for a brief and luminous moment seemed able to do the miraculous: attract the support of frightened, impoverished, desperate blacks, and their angry, in-sistent spokesmen, and, as well, working-class white people, called these days names like "middle Americans," "blue-collar work-ers," "white-collar workers," or, to some extent, members of various "ethnic groups." How did it come about that blacks and whites, the well-to-do and the poor, intellectuals, and ordinary working people, the thoroughly "moderate" (for example, profes-sional politicians within the Democratic party) and the insis-tently activist or radical (among not only blacks, but Chicanos, Appalachian people and Indians), the young and the old, found themselves so drawn to his candidacy?

Again, one comes up with the usual questions. Was it the Kennedy family's aura, which can subdue almost magically so many otherwise conflicting passions? Were Americans in large numbers who felt "guilty" about the assassination of John Ken-nedy hence attracted to his brother as an act of atonement? I find those essentially psychological ways of looking at what has happened in America of little help; sometimes they are flimsy, even vulgar, efforts at "mind reading" that have no firm basis in actual and sustained encounters with the people so sweepingly (and often enough melodramatically) "analyzed." For that mat-ter, many polls can fail to capture and convey the subtleties of thought so many voters, like those who write about them, find themselves struggling with. So much depends on who asks what of whom—and especially asks what in which manner, using which words, phrases, terms. Several of the people I have worked with these past five years have told me that they know what to say to which people; they would not, for instance, in 1968 tell certain people they met how strongly they favored some of George

Wallace's positions, indeed, his candidacy. Sometimes they were not sure until the last minute how they themselves would settle the various sentiments, attitudes and convictions coming at them, it seemed, from all corners of their lives: their past, their present-day experiences, their encounters with friends and neighbors as well as newspapers or television programs.

I cannot in this essay go into an extended analysis of Robert Kennedy's "relationship" with various sections of the American electorate, but I can indicate this on the basis of my own impressions gained from workers like the one I have been quoting here. Maybe I should quote from this man one final time—that is, let *him* indicate what in fact he has taught me: "I liked Robert Kennedy more than any other politician; I liked him even better than his brother, the president. Robert Kennedy was tough; I always admired Jimmy Hoffa, because he was tough and no one could push him around, and he made the Teamsters so strong, but he met his match in Bobby Kennedy. The man had heart; he could really make you feel bigger than yourself (your usual self) when you heard him talk about the colored or those farm workers out there in the West someplace. But he never looked down on you. He never apologized for what he believed in. He didn't let anyone push him around. You could see his heart on his sleeve, but he had a strong arm, and I'll bet he could squeeze your hand real tight, and if he was crossed, I'll bet he knew how to shake his fist back. We used to say in the factory; he's one of us who made good and knows how to think and hasn't lost touch with the ordinary man. I'd hear him talk and the man actually made me believe there was a lot we could do in this country to make it better. With most politicians, you say to yourself: they're no good; they're liars and opportunists, but they could be even worse; so count your blessings. Not with Bobby Kennedy; he knew about the ordinary man, he knew about our ordinary hopes and what we're scared of, our fears, even if they're just ordinary fears— like whether I'll be able to live a halfway respectable life and not die in some poor debtor's prison or owing a lot of rich greedy doctors and hospitals thousands of dollars!"

Bigger than yourself (*your usual self*)—I believe something more than a renowned family's glamour or "charisma" brings about that sense in thousands of people. Of all the condescending remarks made about American working people none excels those that make some people dupes of screen magazines, or gullible, hypnotized victims of fashion photographers, not to mention those endless so-called writers who chronicle the fortunes of families like the Kennedys. There is nothing all that unusual about the man, some of whose views I have tried to set forth. He may even be as thoughtful and analytical as some of us who make rather a show of our ability to reason. He has to make such an effort on the run, so to speak, rather than leisurely or for a living. If I appear to be a little too "defensive" about him and others like him, I am willing to acknowledge the risks that go with an extended "involvement," or "relationship," as it is put these days. Yet, maybe I am "defensive" because I have heard for so long about that man's own "defensiveness," his "narrowness" and "parochialism," his "fascist" susceptibilities.

How *extraordinary*, some of us said, openly or to one another in the privacy of our drawing rooms and libraries, how utterly extraordinary that a Harrisburg jury, made up of such solid, apparently conservative, thoroughly average, hardly cosmopolitan or sophisticated men and women, should have seen through the government's efforts and failed to give them a much-desired sanction. Once again we find it tempting to be rather stingy with our social and psychological analysis; once again we express gratitude for what happened, but no real confidence in the reasons for such a turn of events.

Far be it from me, at this moment in history, to deny anyone's basis for serious reservations about this country and, yes, its people, who like people everywhere have more than occasional moments of greed and callousness. But there *is* another side to all of this, another side to the minds of millions of American working people, who do not live quite the "one-dimensional" lives some theorists (on what basis of actual, firsthand observation?) claim, and who can indeed respond to a Daniel Berrigan, a

Robert Kennedy, a Harrisburg defense team of lawyers and their clients—all of which may not be the news some of us would like to have about "them." Unquestionably, as some of the remarks quoted here illustrate, other responses are also forthcoming from "them," and maybe from "us," too, because liberal and radical intellectuals can also upon occasion prove to be narrow, mean, ungenerous, envious, spiteful. Still, despair is a large sin indeed, and one we are, anyway, in no position to afford right now. The factory worker I have shared this essay with, like the rest of us, has gone through the 1960s with his particular hopes and fears (ordinary ones, as he takes pains to insist) and still shows himself capable of rising to the occasion, rallying around a Robert Kennedy, jumping to Dan Berrigan's side, taking after all sorts of powers and principalities. He can also, I have to remind myself and the reader, vote for a Richard Nixon and come up with some rather mean-spirited observations about his fellowman. As I keep being reminded by him how little leeway he has in this society, and how often he has felt himself and others he feels close to betrayed, I find myself wondering what he might be like were the nation different, were his better side given a wider range of encouragement.

The threat to our society from so-called "domestic" subversion is as serious as any threat from abroad. Never in our history has this country been confronted with so many revolutionary elements determined to destroy by force the government and the society it stands for.

     —Former Attorney General John Mitchell,
      in a speech to the Virginia Bar, 1971

Assuming that it was, if not right, not illegal for the Justice Department to organize its efforts in a campaign against domestic radicalism . . . a critical question remains. Were the defendants tried for committing criminal acts, or was the Justice Department's machinery used to attack people who were exercising their sacred, constitutionally protected rights to wage a war of ideas—an ideological and not a criminal war— about national policy and morality?

         —Ronald L. Goldfarb

Politics at the Justice Department

RONALD L. GOLDFARB

ON HIS ROAD TO THE PRESIDENCY, Richard M. Nixon made one thing, as he liked to say, perfectly clear. He did not appreciate and would not tolerate the antics of the radical peace movement. And to him that loose label included numerous high-profile, well-known personalities and activists in politics and national social action organizations including the Church, along with many simple, relatively invisible individuals who shared some of the symbols and points of view of the organized, doctrinaire radical left, though little of its ideology or its tactics.

Along with official organizations of the radical left, then, young people, street marchers, loud-mouths, long-hairs, crazy clerics, unpatriotic servicemen and ex-servicemen—unconventional, un-businesslike people like these—were anathema to the first Nixon administration. And their shenanigans (the disorder at the 1968 Democratic Convention in Chicago was a perfect example) would provide ammunition, from the first, for the Nixon law and order attack. If campaign followers and media savants wanted to know if there was to be a new Nixon after 1968, on this score he was candid and consistent from the start.

On the hot evening of August 8, 1968, in the Miami Beach, Florida, Convention Hall, addressing a house full of thousands of

Ronald Goldfarb is senior partner of Goldfarb and Singer, a law firm in Washington, D.C. He was a special prosecutor assigned to the organized crime section of the Criminal Division of the Justice Department under Robert Kennedy. A well-known critic of law-enforcement institutions, he is author of *The Contempt Power; Ransom: A Critique of the American Bail System;* (with Alfred Friendly) *Crime and Publicity;* and (with Linda Singer) *After Conviction.*

delegates, alternates, politicos, and conventioneers, and millions of watching and listening Americans, Richard Nixon zeroed in on his target and advised countrymen that he would replace Ramsey Clark as attorney general when elected (as if any incoming President would not choose his own cabinet officers) because he said, "If we are to return order and respect in this country, there is one place we're going to begin. We are going to have a new attorney general of the United States of America." And, in what proved to be a warning reference to the antiwar movement, he told his Republican audience, America's prestige and power abroad was at an unacceptable, all-time low because: "A nation that can't keep the peace at home can't be trusted to keep the peace abroad."

After the election and until the bitter end of its first four-year political lease, the Nixon administration, especially its Justice Department, pursued this upright Nixonian policy guideline with complete and enthusiastic dedication.

One sees this attitude reflected in the comments of administration officials, especially the former vice president, who provided the heavy voice for the president on issues like these, and who seemed to thrive on prosy, rhetorical sallies against "amoral misfits," "obscenity-chanting young dissidents" and their "permissive prattle," the strident minority of protesters who were "long on locks and lean on faith," all of whom composed in his mind the radical movement "which simply cannot survive in a democracy without violence." Agnew frequently spoke about the fearful threat of revolutionary conduct by "kooks and demagogues," outright criminals "who commit their despicable acts against society in the name of political activity."

More particularly, however, it was the high Justice Department officials who led the prosecutorial offensive and provided forensic defense in the growing encounter between government and the antiwar left. One can reconstruct from the public record a continuous process of polarization that steadily drove the protagonists to more extreme positions and actions.[1]

As early as May 1969, the man Nixon chose to replace Clark as attorney general, John Mitchell told a Law Day group in Detroit that growing violence was a threat to the legal system, that "the protest movement has escalated its tactics." He flexed his executive muscles and called for

an end to minority tyranny on the nation's campuses and for the immediate reestablishment of civil peace and the protection of individual rights. If arrests must be made, then arrests there should be. If violators must be prosecuted, then prosecutions there should be. It is no admission of defeat, as some may claim, to use reasonable physical force to eliminate physical force. The price of civil tranquillity cannot be paid by submission to violence and terror.

Later in that speech Mitchell stated his theory of civil disobedience:

In this country, the historical key to civil disobedience has been its amenability to arrest and prosecution. Indeed, it has always been considered, as Thoreau told Emerson, that the moral righteousness of breaking a law was in the punishment that the law meted out.

Today's militants also reject that concept. They physically resist arrest and they are unwilling to submit the merits of their cause to any tribunal other than their own self-determination.

In November 1969, the attorney general in an address in Wisconsin expressed his concern with "the problem of cynicism in America," urging that "an excess of political diversity can be as dangerous as the absence of it," and deplored those "who reject the established political processes and who turn to violence and confrontation."

In September 1970, Mitchell told a student government association meeting in Washington, D.C. that escalating campus violence must be isolated from peaceful demonstrations and other legitimate campus activities, repeating earlier Nixon claims that our system provided peaceful means for change and warnings that "no cause justifies violence in the name of change."

In May 1971, Mitchell told the California Peace Officers Association that law enforcement authorities should not "let the rights

robbers rule their streets" but instead should prosecute the ring-
leaders of these disrupters.

In June 1971, then Deputy, Attorney General Richard Kleindienst assured the Cleveland Rotary Club that spreading mob
violence and "the rule of the anarchistic mob will not prevail in
this country," even if justified in the name of peace and order. He
suggested ominously that the organized disrupters of the antiwar
organizations were "connected with . . . foreign adversary interests," and were "not a group of frolicking picnickers" but part
of a deadly serious, highly organized and mobilized force who
were guilty of "vicious and wanton mob attack," not peaceful,
nonviolent, civil disobedience of the variety epitomized by men of
peace such as Thoreau and Martin Luther King.

In June 1971, Mitchell advised the Virginia Bar Association
how seriously he viewed the protest movement:

The threat to our society from so-called "domestic" subversion is
as serious as any threat from abroad. Never in our history has this
country been confronted with so many revolutionary elements determined to destroy by force the Government and the society it stands
for. These "domestic" forces are ideologically and in many instances
directly connected with foreign interests.

Mitchell detailed the increasing acts of sabotage, terrorist bombings occurring in the country, and called for more prosecutive
powers to assure national security. The then Internal Security
Chief Robert Mardian repeated this concern about increasing acts
of sabotage in a speech to the Ninth Judicial Circuit in June
1971. Their statistics were frightening; their point about the
dangers of violence was a fair one; only their solutions were
highly questionable.

In April 1972, then Assistant Attorney General L. Patrick
Gray, later acting FBI director, told the South Carolina Educa-
tional Association in tough, proud language how the administration had cut lawlessness in the country including "the use of
destruction, disruption, murder, and riot planned and executed to
achieve political goals. I am not referring to peaceful assemblies

and demonstrations, which are and must be protected by the Constitution. I am referring to criminal acts which are no less criminal when it is contended that they are performed in further-ance of a cause alleged to be political."

During this same four-year period, J. Edgar Hoover, whose FBI was administratively a part of the Department of Justice but politically was a force parallel to and often greater than its parent, was vocal in his constant disparagement of the antiwar movement. No discussion of the politics of the Justice Depart-ment would be complete without mention of the unhidden fact of life that the FBI had its own politics which often were distinct from those of the department itself. In the present context, however, the FBI's policies were not different from those of the department; in fact, the bureau was in front of the department's battle lines.

In a steady stream of articles in PTA, Veterans of Foreign Wars, law enforcement organization magazines; in law reviews; in his regular testimony before friendly congressional appropria-tions subcommittees—the FBI's equivalent of corporate annual reports to stockholders—the director chronicled the dangers of the radical antiwar movement. Hoover assured all who would listen that the FBI was constantly on the alert to check the excesses of "New Left extremism."

Hoover deplored as a serious danger to national security the "power of the fanatical few" to disrupt, destroy and endanger the rights, lives, and property of others. He compared the old-style, Baby Face Nelson hoodlums to the new breed of "arrogant," "ruthless," frequently Marxist "revolutionary guerrillas" whose criminal acts are public, violent, and "designed to tear down society as a whole"; they were, in his words, "the Attilas or Luddites of contemporary society." The idealism and legitimate questioning of many antiwar people has been manipulated, "dis-torted or even lost in the maelstrom of the New Left's excesses and extremist acts," Hoover admonished. It was his opinion that these extremists were bent on "overthrow of democratic institutions," and that, in fact, "the dangerous Rubicon of violence had been crossed."

How repulsive he found the style and cosmetics of the New Left is evident in Hoover's colorful rhetoric as he described their "neopaganism," "Trotskyite" mannerisms, the "nauseating air of self-righteousness" displayed by these "rhetoric-mongers" and "intellectual tramps who seek the exotic and eccentric as emotional outlets" and preach a "gospel of nihilism." Hoover conjured all these pieces together to compose this conspiratorial picture:

The time has come for Americans to focus on a new kind of conspiracy in our country—a movement called the New Left. In recent months the effects of the New Left have been seen in many places: in demonstrations against American policy in Viet Nam, in civil disobedience, in calls for young men to resist the draft, in campus turmoil, in attacks against law and order, in desecrations of the American flag.

What is the New Left? . . .

Most of the participants are students. The New Left is predominantly a college-age movement found in the college and university community—but not exclusively. Besides undergraduates, the New Left contains a wide assortment of other participants: college faculty members (mostly young), graduate students, guitarists, writers, intellectuals of various types, ex-students still "hanging around" the campus, curiosity-seekers, Communists, Trotskyites.

And, in the following remarks, Hoover displayed how close he viewed the line to be between crime and protest:

There is in today's campus turbulence a new style in conspiracy—conspiracy that is extremely subtle and devious and hence difficult to understand. It is a conspiracy reflected by questionable moods and attitudes, by unrestrained individualism, by nonconformism in dress and speech, even by obscene language, rather than by formal membership in specific organizations.

Often called the New Left, this conspiracy has unloosed disrespect for the law, contempt for our institutions for free government, and disdain for spiritual and moral values.

The pressures on both sides built up to the point where, at least as a matter of hindsight, some public eruption was inevitable. While the left was calling the country a fascistic Amerika, the right was calling the antiwar movement an anarchistic revolution. Hoover and the Berrigans became representatives of two extreme views of the country, its political morality, its social temperature, its ideological direction. Each moved his constituency further than it might have gone naturally; Hoover pushed the indictment of the Berrigans; the Berrigans and their followers escalated their forms of protest in the cause of peace.

Both sides did what they thought had to be done, taking progressively more active steps. In the case of the antiwar movement, the direction was from teach-ins, to pray-ins, to silent vigils, to large street demonstrations, to draft-card burning, to draft board rip-offs, trashings, bombings, etc.; on Hoover's part, to press within the administration for the surveillance, investigation, and ultimately the indictment of movement leaders. Similarly, each side rationalized its positions and steps with moral rhetoric; each said its purpose was to save America, to do what was right and true. Probably, too, each lost some credibility and authenticity, except in its own camp. And, it is now clear, each played into the other's prejudices and positions so that accommodation became impossible; a collision became inevitable.

The first public hint of the Harrisburg case received very little attention. On September 23, 1970, Scripps-Howard staff writer Dan Thomasson published a story about a forty-five minute White House briefing of Republican congressional leaders the day before by President Nixon, Attorney General Mitchell and FBI Director Hoover. The purpose of the briefing, according to Thomasson, was to make a pitch for additional funds to hire 1,000 new FBI agents and for new legislative authority for the Justice Department and FBI to investigate campus violence. At the meeting, this report added, Hoover advised congressional leaders that a group calling itself the East Coast Conspiracy to Save Lives had plans to "bomb sewers and conduits in the District of Columbia and to kidnap political leaders in an attempt to win release of leftist colleagues now in prison and to obtain other political concessions."

Jim Wieghart, the Washington correspondent for the *New York Daily News*, also had heard about this meeting and reported on October 15, 1970 that Hoover had briefed the president and congressional leaders at a private White House meeting on September 22, 1970 that there were dangers of a political kidnaping or assassination. Hoover warned that "a new secret revolutionary group, called the East Coast Conspiracy to Save Lives planned . . . to plant bombs in strategic places in the capital city . . . in order to cripple communities," according to Wieghart.

Around that time there had been reports of terrorist kidnapings of public officials in Canada and Uruguay, and of skyjackings by Palestinian guerillas. When Wieghart questioned Justice Department spokesmen about the high-level meeting, he was informed that it was scuttlebutt; that there was nothing very serious to worry about.

No one picked up on either of these two stories at the time. When I questioned one Senate aide who was there about Wieghart's report of the meeting between Hoover and Senate GOP leadership, he could not remember who requested the meeting, where it was held, or even what was said. He did recall that Hoover's announcement did not make much impact, was just informative, and that "everyone went away feeling better."

According to a recent article by Jack Anderson, on September 4, 1970 (several weeks before the meeting mentioned above), Hoover had sent a secret letter to presidential adviser Henry Kissinger informing him that he had been mentioned as a possible "kidnap victim." A few months earlier, White House aide John Ehrlichman and the Secret Service had been notified by Hoover about the alleged plans to destroy underground utilities in Washington. The Secret Service had investigated the charge and had found no information to confirm that plot.

Then, in his now-famous statement to a closed-door Senate appropriations subcommittee on November 27, 1970 (copies of the same testimony delivered a week earlier to a House subcommittee were made public at the same time), Hoover got specific about these charges and included in his analysis of New Left terrorism, this explosive announcement:

Willingness to employ any type of terrorist tactics is becoming increasingly apparent among extremist elements. One example has recently come to light involving an incipient plot on the part of an anarchist group on the east coast, the so-called East Coast Conspiracy to Save Lives.

This is a militant group self-described as being composed of Catholic priests and nuns, teachers, students, and former students who have manifested opposition to the war in Vietnam by acts of violence against Government agencies and private corporations engaged in work relating to U.S. participation in the Vietnam conflict.

The principal leaders of this group are Philip and Daniel Berrigan, Catholic priests who are currently incarcerated in the Federal Correctional Institution at Danbury, Conn., for their participation in the destruction of Selective Service Records in Baltimore, Md., in 1968.

This group plans to blow up underground electrical conduits and steam pipes serving the Washington, D.C., area in order to disrupt Federal Government operations. The plotters are also concocting a scheme to kidnap a highly placed Government official. The name of a White House staff member has been mentioned as a possible victim. If successful, the plotters would demand an end to U.S. bombing operations in Southeast Asia and the release of all political prisoners as ransom. Intensive investigation is being conducted concerning this matter.

The announcement caused widespread reactions. At a hurriedly called press conference, lawyers denied Hoover's charges. The Berrigans issued a statement from prison stating that in view of the seriousness of Hoover's allegations, the goverment should be made "either to prosecute us or publicly retract the charges he has made."

Finally, on January 12, 1971, a grand jury in Harrisburg, Pennsylvania indicted Eqbal Ahmad, Philip Berrigan, Elizabeth McAlister, Neil McLaughlin, Anthony Scoblick, Joseph Wenderoth for conspiracy to kidnap and illegal traffic in contraband at a federal correctional institution. The die was now cast, and speculation abounded whether this case was a political persecution or the vindication of Hoover's long-felt fears about the Berrigans and their antiwar politics.

Writing about past cases makes for stale drama, especially when the situation has had the extensive and prolonged press coverage that this one has had. Indeed, two savvy investigative newspaper reporters, Jack Nelson and Ronald Ostrow, have written a thorough and absorbing book about the case which leaves few available facts undigested.[2] I shall mention only some facts about the case here because they focus on two profound questions: was the case a political trial and just what does that provocative term mean?

The attorney general was a very political man. One point of view, one he did little to discourage, was that John Mitchell's lodestone—his number one goal from the moment he began his attorney generalship until the moment he ended it—was the reelection of Richard Nixon. In the opinion of one of his aides at the time, "that was his primary view of every issue that came before the Justice Department." Mitchell had determined from the beginning of his reign at Justice that placating J. Edgar Hoover was crucial, and that a happy, indulgent working relationship with him would be best. Understanding Hoover's power over his men, minions, and fans all over the country, Mitchell feared him, and decided that the best way to control the FBI was to kill Hoover with kindness. For this he paid a heavy price, but it worked; I was told, "their relationship was just great."

One Justice Department official at the time speculated to me that Mitchell was not the "the evil genius" in the Berrigan case. In fact, he said, the key attitude in the Justice Department was "don't look for political trouble"; and indicting the Berrigans would lead to political trouble. The Nixon administraton, he reminded, did not need "any more Brownie points from the right wing, and there was a lot of risk in bringing this case." What probably happened, in this official's opinion, was that Hoover, who hated the Berrigans and the antiwar movement, simply went to Congress and "turned the screws."

The case also played into another less important, but complementary, behind-the-scenes game of political musical chairs that was going on in the Justice Department at that time. Robert C. Mardian had been eased out of his job as general counsel of HEW, reportedly because of his civil rights positions which angered co-workers who saw him as a reactionary force in their midst.

Mardian was a good friend of Richard Kleindienst who had brought him to the Justice Department. He was described to me by a Justice Department official at the time as a "very smart, right-winger." Mardian's political past being what it was (he had campaigned for Goldwater and Nixon), it was necessary to create a job for him that seemed important and none was available.

It was decided that the answer to the Mardian employment problem was to glamorize the then moribund Internal Security Division and put Mardian in charge. His predecessor was made a local judge. Until Mardian came to Justice, the Internal Security Division was so atrophied and out of business, that in the words of one old department hand, "you could hear a pin drop."

Mardian was led to believe that there would be a lot to do if he took over the division, that he would be in control of a lot of important cases; in fact, the hint was made that he would be made deputy attorney general when Mitchell left and Kleindienst climbed to the top post.[3]

Justice William Rehnquist admitted in a conversation in his chambers recently that while he was not party to any of the decision-making processes regarding the Berrigan trial, he was aware that there had been a transfer of jurisdiction from the Criminal Division to the Internal Security Division when Mardian took over the job. Draft prosecutions, for example, were brought under the jurisdiction of the Internal Security Division by order of the attorney general. These draft cases, the "stepchild" of the Justice Department, were given more impetus in the Internal Security Division, where, in effect, they were big fish in a small pond. The move of the Selective Service cases from the Criminal Division to Internal Security was made, in the words of one high Criminal Division attorney, "with a sigh of relief," since they were "ghastly" cases to prosecute.

While the Internal Security Division's Guy Goodwin first conducted the Berrigan case investigation as the attorney in charge (according to Nelson and Ostrow however, until Hoover's testimony the case was being investigated under the direction of the Criminal Division[4]), it soon became clear that a substantial trial lawyer was needed by the government in this case. Richard Kleindienst called William Lynch, who was then chief of the organized crime section and one of the best trial lawyers in the department, to his office and told him that they wanted him to try the case. At the time, Lynch, a career lawyer, very much a behind-the-scenes man, and not a political personality, was more interested in his organized crime work which was going well. He really did not want this case; it was not his personal priority.

Nevertheless, Lynch promised Kleindienst that he would review the case and give him a decision on the merits. After closeting himself for several days in his Alexandria townhouse to study all the papers, Lynch decided there was a case and, good public servant that he is (and always craving another good trial as all trial lawyers do), Lynch agreed to try it if substantive changes he felt necessary were made. Some unindicted co-conspirators (including Daniel Berrigan) had to be dropped from the January 1971 indictment; some defendants had to be added, and the main charge had to be changed from the offense of conspiracy to kidnap (life sentence) to general conspiracy (five years).

More grand jury work ensued. Three months later a superseding indictment accomplished these changes. It left the letter-smuggling charges essentially the same, but two key letters between Fr. Philip Berrigan and Sr. Elizabeth McAlister were attached to the new indictment, giving vast and presumably prejudicial public exposure to the key communication discussing the fantasy or plan to kidnap Kissinger and bomb tunnels, as well as to the warm relationship between the two clergy.

In Lynch's mind, it was important to show that these defendants were not peaceful, sweet, antiwar people who would have been unlikely to commit so serious and personal a crime as kidnaping. These were people, in his mind, who had escalated their antiwar protests from peaceful, nonviolent activities to ripping-off draft boards, and who were both sophisticated in their techniques and quite capable of accelerating their activities to the degree charged in the conspiracy count of the indictment. Lynch pointed out to me that some of the defendants had raided three draft boards in one night and done it so well that they even had advised the FBI ahead of time that it would happen and still had gotten away with it. Thus, the indictment was changed to show the evolution of "competent saboteurs."

According to Lynch, the decision about the case was totally apolitical. "I had no personal reasons to beg off the case or to want it. My only question here, as in all cases, was, is it prosecutable? When I decided that it was, I agreed to handle it," he told me. The indictment was changed to make it a more careful, less shoot-from-the-hip prosecution, according to him.

The prosecutorial machinery Hoover had set in motion the Justice Department had to control. Lynch led the prosecutorial team now, and Ramsey Clark the defense. The trial was from all perspectives an unsatisfying encounter. In observer Garry Wills' words, it was "a play of shadows . . . each side more interested in cutting its losses than in winning. . . . The government was ashamed of its own chief witness, and the defense was afraid to put anyone on the stand." Courtroom histrionics were avoided; both sides played to win the case, not to put on a show. The verdict, which in effect freed the defendants of all charges except for the smuggling of letters, was considered widely as their effective exoneration.

There always have been and there always will be political elements in the administration of justice in the United States. Yet, the differences between administrations of the Justice Department

often are vast because both in its prosecutorial and in its investigative work *there are politics and there are politics.* There are
politics of the partisan variety and politics of a more philosophical kind, having to do with prosecutorial discretion and the
setting of internal administrative priorities. Defining in some
measure these two "political" elements helps one to understand
the workings of any particular Justice regime.

In 1961, when I was in the Kennedy Justice Department, an
incident occurred which demonstrates the inevitability of the party-
politics element in the administration of justice. As a young
attorney in the department, I was sent to investigate and later to
prosecute a notorious case in Kentucky. The trial involved the
drugging and false arrest of former football star, George Ratterman, who at the time was running as a reform candidate for
sheriff, pledged to clean up Newport, long one of the country's
classic sin cities and a prime target in Robert F. Kennedy's
organized crime drive. The case took on national proportions
because of the notoriety of the town, the celebrity status of
Ratterman, and the drama of the incident. (Ratterman, father of
nine, from a respected local family with one brother an FBI agent
and another a priest, had been arrested in bed with a stripper.)

The reformers, many of whom were tied to local church groups,
pressed the Justice Department to take action against the people
who they claimed had framed Ratterman. The local sheriff's election was coming up; it was their first real chance to clean up
Newport; they could not afford skepticism about their candidate's
compromising predicament.

A long investigation by the grand jury and FBI was necessary
before a departmental judgment could be made whether a federal
offense had been committed. The press and many Ratterman-
reform detractors began speculating that since there was no
indictment, obviously, Ratterman was not clean and his posture
as a reformer was laughable.

The lawyers who were conducting the case eventually recommended prosecution. Because the case was one of unique legal
posture, difficult to prove, politically hot, and in the limelight,

Kennedy was particularly careful in his considerations before approving the proposed indictment. I remember arguing with him and other high officials of the Justice Department that we had a case and recommending that we be allowed to prosecute it.

At this point Kennedy expressed concern about charges that the forthcoming indictment was politically motivated—an attempt to interject Kennedy politics into a local sheriff's election—that an indictment of Ratterman's enemies implicitly would be a political endorsement of Ratterman.

I argued that Kennedy could not avoid political overtones in the case; they were inevitable. Indeed, I pointed out, if he did approve the indictment, no doubt the charge against him would be made; however, if he did *not* approve the indictment, the charge would be made, advantageous to the other side, that there was no case and therefore Ratterman and his reform candidacy were condemned by the Justice Department. In other words, the attorney general could not avoid politics, whichever way he decided.[5]

There have been more obvious, grosser examples of politicians clashing with the prosecutorial machinery of Justice. When I was in the department, a colleague proposed the indictment of the mayor of Gary, Indiana—a Democrat with strong party connections who had been helpful in the John F. Kennedy campaign and who was Ambassador-designate to Greece at the time of his indictment—at no small embarrassment to the attorney general's brother, the president!

As a matter of fact, the top political animals in the Kennedy administration helplessly watched Robert Kennedy's organized crime drive knock off politician after politician around the country, most of whom were Democrats. In one regular meeting in Robert Kennedy's office, the lawyers in the organized crime section sat around informally and described the cases they were working on in different cities. One lawyer after another reported the political corruption scalps he was gathering. Robert Kennedy —sleeves rolled up, tie loosened, fingers together in front of his face, listened to the reports, asking questions here and there, including inevitably, "Was he Republican or Democrat?" One after another, the lawyers reported to him: "Democrat." After three or four such exchanges he commented with a smile, "If you guys keep this up my brother is going to have to take me out of here and send me to the Supreme Court."

The point is that the fairest, most detached attorney general—the most unpolitical Justice Department—cannot avoid the presence of political factors in the decision-making process. The issue then is not whether, but to what extent and in what ways politics should be a concern of the national prosecutor's office.

As the political power of the attorney general is great, so is the need to keep it in check. From the first Judiciary Act in 1789 to the formal creation of the Department of Justice almost a century later (in 1870), Congress feared an increase in the attorney general's powers and remained reluctant to concentrate legal decisions for all executive departments in the attorney general's office. Members of Congress also feared the loss of their influence on the appointment of district judges, U.S. marshals, U.S. attorneys.

As a result, until 1870, the primary functions of the attorney general were argument in the Supreme Court (now done almost independently by the solicitor general and his small, select group of young assistants), and the formulation of advisory opinions for the president and other executive officers. Direct responsibility for federal law enforcement was denied.

Presently, the attorney general has the job of picking federal district attorneys and judges; this involves the ticklish task of coordinating decision making with local political operatives and Congress. Inevitably, he is subject to party political pressures in matters like these. His prosecutorial judgments are subject to more subtle pressures in matters which may run the gamut from outright attempts at bribery or influence peddling to unethical pressures to bring or drop a tax case against a certain powerful individual, to halt a proposed antitrust prosecution against some influential company under investigation, to get the Civil Rights Division out of a given southern county, to indict or not to indict an individual who has served and financed his party long and well.[6]

One last, perhaps paradoxical, point on this subject. It is not correct to assume that a political attorney general is a low quality or venal official simply because he was appointed to his job because of his political power rather than his brain power. Robert F. Kennedy did not get to be attorney general as the culmination of an illustrious career as a legal scholar or practitioner. Nonetheless, despite his ascension to high government power through solely political and nepotistic avenues, he went on to become an excellent, independent attorney general. Ironically, because he was who he was, politically he could act with unusual sureness and power; but he used this extra power in very substantial and admirable ways.

By comparison, others came to the attorney generalship with exceptional academic backgrounds and after considerable high-level experience in the bar and in government service—only to be docile, ineffective attorneys general because their tenuous and uncertain relationships with their presidents and other sources of political power left them without the strength and assertiveness necessary for an attorney general to do great things.

One's political position, then, should not be viewed as solely a hindrance to or disqualification from greatness as attorney general; in fact, if the right balance can be struck, political strength is a necessity for a great attorney general. Politically powerful attorneys general do not have to capitulate to political considerations to the degree politically weak ones do. As one very high Nixon appointee said to me about John Mitchell: "Our boss had more political clout than any pol who came in and tried to press us, so we didn't have to bend to political pressures." Others would say that no political figure should be attorney general; that Robert Kennedy and John Mitchell were dangerous precedents.

About party line politics, one can only say that the best Justice Department should do as much as possible to eliminate this element from its administration. Nonetheless, the problem of its presence inheres in the nature of the institution, and history demonstrates that its existence is not exclusively characteristic of either political party. The balance between politics and the administration of justice is a constant dynamic, to be kept firmly in mind in judging the workings of any Justice Department.

While the Nixon administration identified with and had its constituency among the forces reacting against the radical antiwar movement, the Berrigan case cannot be called a political trial in the partisan, party politics sense of that term. It was a highly visible example of the department's work that must have been popular to Nixon's political constituency; but it could not be called a party-politics case.

Difficult and elusive as it is to define the proper role of party politics in the Justice Department, questions involving a second kind of politics at the federal level are even more profound and perplexing. The Berrigan case—*U.S. v. Ahmad, et al.,* as it is formally captioned (that the case is commonly referred to in the name of its most political and notorious member is a measure of its politicalization in the public's mind)—was a dramatic illustration of the phenomenon of prosecutorial priority making by the Nixon Justice Department; it was a symbolic example of that department's emphasis of law enforcement policy.

The formation of prosecutorial policies, however, is the task of the department. Each Justice Department focuses on special areas of interest depending on the issues to which the newly elected administration directed attention in its election campaign, the exigencies thrust upon it by times and events over which it has little control, and the predilections of the men who run it. Policy judgments and institutional emphases are the political statements of attorneys general, presidents, and administrations; they compose a vital form of the exercise of sovereign power.

Clearly, the Nixon administration was concerned about such areas of social action as student riots, draft resistance and organized antiwar resistance—the thunder from the left. As a result of this well-advertised institutional, philosophic concern, it should have come as no surprise to anyone that the Justice Department would take an active part. The prosecution of the Chicago Seven opened the Mitchell regime at Justice; the mass arrests of war protesters in Washington D.C. highlighted it; and the Berrigan trial came as a late showing that despite little support in the courts, the department was undeterred in its zeal in this area.

This concern was apparent in isolated, petty administrative actions as well as in broad prosecutorial policies; in the hiring of recruits in the department as well as in court appointments. But, as the key ingredient in characterizing a Justice Department regime usually is provided by its *causes célèbres*, its few notorious trials; so were the Nixon years at Justice epitomized by the handling of this unusual case.

In political trials of any definition, elements of discretion—often exercised at a high level—become critical. A notorious case may arouse great public pressures to indict while the judgment of the prosecutor is that proof simply is not there. He may be sure an offense was committed but uncertain, due to circumstances surrounding the case, whether a jury would convict.

Does he exercise caution and not unleash the prosecutive machinery without a high degree of certainty that a conviction will follow? Does he take the attitude that justice is what the jury says, present his case, and leave it to the jury? Does he take an aggressive stance and prosecute a case because his judgment is that, whatever may be the verdict, the nature of the offense or of the defendant demands that any possible case be brought, regardless of the results?

Questions like these arise in regular, if relatively infrequent, situations. However much we may profess to be a government of law and not of men, it is impossible to eliminate all personal judgmental elements of prosecutive discretion. Obvious cases are the easy ones to decide; provocative ones are those where arguments and pressures on both sides are persuasive. All prosecutors, then, within the bounds of law and ethics and morals, must concern themselves with which cases are brought and which are not.

Prosecutorial discretion is inevitable and precipitous. Former Attorney General and Supreme Court Justice Robert Jackson once stated: "The prosecutor has more control over life, liberty, and reputation than any other person in America." But this awesome power is not boundless; the system is not without checks on these sovereign powers.[7] Prosecutors cannot indict for serious cases without the approval of a grand jury. Although it is rare for a grand jury to second-guess a prosecutor, it is a classical function of the jury to serve as an insulation between the public and the overzealous prosecutor; on at least some occasions that function is exercised. Judges can dismiss cases which have been brought improvidently. Juries may not agree and thus may forestall a verdict, or they may ignore the prosecutor and find a defendant not guilty. Appellate courts can overrule convictions based on questionable legal foundations, such as a federal court did in the famous Spock case. The chief executive can commute or pardon a sentence even where guilt was found.

While institutional restraints on abusive prosecution may provide small solace to a person indicted improvidently and thus forced to undergo the arduous process of self-defense at a criminal trial, at least it must be remembered that the mighty power of the prosecutor is not absolute. He is constrained by the dynamics of internal administrative balancing, by external institutional checks, and, finally, by public opinion.

Prosecutors are limited as well by the sheer volume of matters under their jurisdiction. It is impossible to tabulate exactly how many cases the Justice Department oversees each year. Informed officials estimate that in the Criminal Division alone about 42,000 matters are considered annually in Washington, ranging from full-scale investigations to simple telephonic inquiries from around the country. This number does not include matters considered by other divisions in the department, and it is only a small fraction (an experienced source estimated between one-tenth and one-twentieth) of matters considered locally in districts where the largest number of federal cases are initiated and handled.

Thus, the vast part of prosecutorial discretion is used as a sort of low level, institutional filter through which a mass of routine complaints around the country are converted into the relative few which ultimately become criminal cases. This kind of unchecked administrative discretion is characteristic of all agencies of government,[8] but oddly has come under less scrutiny and questioning in the Justice Department than elsewhere.

A case may be filed by police with a U.S. attorney; a complaint may be made by a citizen to the FBI; the IRS computer might crank out a tax return that smells wrong; a grand jury may turn up a lead in the course of its investigations. Such cases are handled by the bureaucrats of the federal prosecutive establishment in a rather perfunctory, mechanical, and impersonal fashion. The attorney general and his chief assistants, to say nothing of other high administrative officials, may hear nothing about any aspect of these cases.

In a speech to the Arizona Law School in April 1970, Justice (then Assistant Attorney General) William H. Rehnquist made the following point in contrasting the Ramsey Clark and John Mitchell regimes at the Justice Department:

I believe that if one were to examine and to compare the actions taken by the Justice Department under these two administrations, one would find that 95% of the business of the Department is being handled today precisely the way it was two years ago. But it is not this 95% that makes news, or makes even reasonably interesting speeches.

The mass of cases may provide a more meaningful description of the work of the Justice Department in the eyes of historians; but in a more political, more parochial, and more important present sense, it is the notorious few cases which not only dramatize but characterize that agency.

The Nixon Justice Department's rejuvenation of the Internal Security Division to conduct criminal trials of antiwar radicals reflected a shift of emphasis, an example of the kind of political policy making that revealed the philosophical sense of the department at this time. And the Berrigan prosecution became the epitome of that division's new lease on life in the Justice Department hierarchy.

There are no immutable laws about administrative classifications. Fifteen years ago, there were a few civil rights lawyers working at Justice; now there is a Civil Rights Division playing a major role in the department. Neither the department's Internal Security Division nor its organized crime section existed from the beginning. Rather, their birth and growth reflected the changing fashions, interests, and priorities of given times.

An Internal Security Division existed in 1970 because internal security had been a major concern of the Justice Department during preceding decades. The division was bolstered both by the FBI's voluminous information in the field and by the Subversive Activities Control Board, which for close to a decade had been effectively out of business, but which the Nixon administration resuscitated.

The Department of Justice historically has taken sporadic but intensive ventures into this area of federal law enforcement. These periodic excursions range from the prosecution of Aaron Burr for treason through treason indictments of the Civil War period and the "red raids" of Woodrow Wilson's attorney general, A. Mitchell Palmer, in 1919. The latter, run by the attorney general, assisted by William J. Flynn's new General Intelligence Division (a predecessor of the FBI), involved the arrest of more than 5,000 individuals as anarchist-syndicalists.

The Communist scare of the McCarthy era livened public interest again in internal security matters. Business was good in the division. Then, in the early 1960s, public disinfatuation with the red scare combined with critical court decisions that emasculated the statutory powers upon which the division's work was based.

The Internal Security Division had been christened, staffed, and funded as a major branch of Justice in 1954. The realities of the Justice Department's administrative charts simply had not changed in 1970 to reflect the change in the facts of life in America. The division was there, reflecting a rear-view mirror of the issues of the times; but its day-to-day business in fact had dried up.[9]

In contrast, organized crime as a special area of federal law enforcement is relatively new: developing on the heels of the Kefauver Senate hearings of the 1950s, it had not become a major emphasis of Justice Department work until Robert Kennedy became attorney general. Then, the section (a part of the Criminal Division) grew from a handful of careerists to a full complement of over fifty lawyers. Kennedy brought in trial lawyers from outside of the government and gave them extraordinary authority, allowing them to operate in a major way. Under President Johnson, Attorneys General Katzenbach and Clark kept up the war on organized crime, as did John Mitchell. That section now has over one hundred lawyers who last year secured 1,012 indictments, compared to a grand total of forty-nine in 1961.

There was talk during the Kennedy and Johnson administrations of phasing down the Internal Security Division to a small section and making the organized crime section a division to reflect better the realities of that time. That administrative change never occurred and, as issues change with the times, the work of the Internal Security Division became a big interest of the Mitchell Justice Department.

The FBI is the culmination of a series of experiments in investigation. Although a small appropriation was provided for this purpose in 1871, the department made do with borrowed Secret Servicemen, "special detectives," and temporary "agents" until 1878. In that year, a staff of internal investigators was created to monitor the accounts of U.S. attorneys, clerks of court, marshals and commissioners. In 1907, Attorney General Charles J. Bonaparte got congressional appropriations to establish the first federal bureau of criminal identification and classification.

President Theodore Roosevelt charged that congressional resistance to a full-fledged federal investigative agency was prompted by fear of their own investigation. But such an organization, the

Bureau of Investigation, was created by President Taft's executive order in 1909. Statutory authority to carry arms, to serve process, and to execute searches and arrests came later in 1934, as a result of J. Edgar Hoover's remarkable exploitation of public interest in sensational criminal cases. His continuing indomitable ability to maintain and expand his extraordinary powers is now a legend. It is well known that the FBI, while on paper a part of the Justice Department and under the direction of the attorney general, often has appeared to be the tail that wagged the departmental dog.

While the essence of the charges in the Berrigan trial were representative of the Nixon administration's policies and prosecutorial priorities at Justice, the administration of the case was highly unusual and questionable. There were numerous evidences of administrative confusion wrought by the case. The FBI announced the case before there was one; the investigation continued after the indictment; the Internal Security Division controlled the case although it involved Criminal Division statutes; the star trial lawyer of the Criminal Division tried the case, though ordinarily divisional pride and jealousy would have precluded such an incursion; and after a long and expensive ordeal the jury would not swallow the serious charges that were the crux of the government's case but did convict some defendants for an exotic offense based on an obscure criminal statute that never before had been invoked.

The Berrigan case then was a political trial in the sense that it represented an emphasis of departmental work, and it was handled in such an unusual way administratively as to indicate a reach to prosecute that went beyond ordinary prosecutorial preference.

If the case was a political trial in the preceding sense, was it so in the way that the term is used by the general public? Lately, the cry "political trial" has been bandied about loosely as a pejorative slogan; I have found only subjective and highly personal understandings of what those words really mean. Current, increasing references to political trials do not mean the partisan, political party affairs which I first described. In fact, the phrase "political trial" has become a term of art which, while it does not exactly embrace the second category of political trials described, does come closest to the class of cases reflecting prosecutors' priorities.

By describing a case as a political trial, the general public seems to mean those regular but infrequent, extraordinary cases which, because of the special people and circumstances involved, take on proportions greater than life. These cases, usually pregnant with emotional and symbolic issues, are only sometimes decisive of them. Their inherently fascinating characters and events generate wide and intensive press coverage; the parties become household names; the issues (often collateral issues raised by the handling of the case which have become more important than those giving rise to the basic dispute itself) are widely discussed. The trials usually involve deep ideological disputes, frequently pitting powers of the state against the unpopular words or deeds of charismatic and vocal defendants. Parochial and subsidiary issues may eclipse the truth about the facts in dispute; the pursuit of justice is confused, sometimes waylaid by engaging and volatile skirmishes along the way.

There is a confusing tendency on the part of protagonists on the right and the left to characterize their cases as political trials, cases brought not on their specific merits but to harass defendants for ideologies or general dangers they represent. Congressman John Dowdy saw his trial as a plot by his enemies, "homosexuals, urban renewal interests and the members of the Eastern liberal establishment" no less than Angela Davis felt her indictment was an antiblack, antiCommunist frame-up by the powerbrokers of a corrupt Amerika. With a wave of one's metaphorical wand, a case takes on proportions greater than the interests of the immediate participants, and the decision about alleged criminal acts is deflected while attention is directed instead to the motives of the defendant and the government. Thus, while some people have been harassed and unjustly prosecuted; others have taken refuge in the suspect countercharge that all actions against them are "politically" motivated.

It might well be a political trial, in the sense often charged, for an antiwar spokesman to be indicted for what he said or advocated or wrote, or even for some strained criminal charge evolving from speech or writings or associations, such as I believe was done in the notorious Chicago Seven case. The exercise of constitutional rights, however unpopular or unpleasant, should never be converted into a criminal act.[10]

On the other hand, it is too great a jump to say that a person indicted for acts in and of themselves criminal by objective standards should be excused from the consequences of those acts simply because he happens to be, say, an author, political leader, or member of the clergy. It is one thing for a demonstrator to argue that the war is unjust and should be stopped; legally, it is quite another for him to destroy property, hurt people, kidnap to make his point. Once he has crossed that line, the fact that his purpose may be highly moral, that his acts are committed in support of an idea which in itself is constitutionally protected is no legal excuse. As Prosecutor Lynch said to me: "Political people don't get a pass" when it comes to prosecutions for crimes.

Justice William H. Rehnquist attempted to delineate this distinction in one speech when, as assistant attorney general, he argued that the Chicago Seven case was *not* a political trial:

Just as one's beliefs cannot and should not afford the basis of any criminal prosecution, one's beliefs cannot and should not guarantee immunity from criminal prosecution for acts which have been made criminal by law. No one may be put in jail for his beliefs, but no one is protected against a jail sentence solely because of his beliefs. The test in every case is whether the defendant has performed acts which are criminally punishable. . . . The fact that the incitation occurred in a political context is not a ground for singling them out for prosecution, but neither is it a ground for refusing to prosecute if the evidence otherwise warrants.

In the Berrigan case, the defendants were not looking for a political trial. They denied doing or planning to do personal

violence in the cause of antiwar protest. They did not espouse any
right to be beyond punishment for criminal acts committed in
support of their views.[11] To have done so would have been to
consider high moral purposes not as mitigation of one's criminal
acts, but as condonation of them. Additionally, the Berrigan
defendants wanted neither to be tried (as Dr. Spock had, and
indeed as the two Berrigan brothers had in the more confessional
Catonsville trial), nor even to use their trial for political purposes
(thus did they replace William Kunstler with less flamboyant
counsel and waive their rights to participate in a political defense
in order to improve their chances for acquittal). The defendants'
defense in the Berrigan case and the jury's disposition of the case
distinguished the group's position from that of others, in the
antiwar movement who have claimed that the whole system is so
corrupt that their criminal acts in protest of it should not be
considered criminal.

If the Berrigan case is deemed political in the sense that it represented a focus of prosecutorial attention during this particular
administration, was loaded with public interest, and was treated
by all the participants as a public challenge between representatives of fundamentally divergent points of view, can critical
inquiry end there? It is not sufficient to say that prosecutorial
pursuit of any course of criminal conduct should be accepted as
an inevitability of government. Difficult as they are to ask, let
alone answer, further questions remain about the limits of prosecutorial discretion. Some principles are needed to provide bounds
and limitations to confine the powers of the prosecutor. Further
inquiry can be raised regarding the legitimacy of a criminal case
when the charge is made that it is a political trial.

A prosecutor may decide that an Al Capone is a dangerous
enough citizen to warrant concentrated attention. That may be a
political judgment in terms of his subjective priority setting. A
legitimate exercise of that discretion, no doubt, would be to bring
an intensive investigation into his criminal escapades and even-

tually to indict him for racketeering, if it could be proved. It also might be legitimate to bring a proper tax case against him, even though the gist of the government's initial concern was not his tax offenses, but his other criminal activity.

On the other hand, the government obviously would not be warranted in bringing a totally contrived case against a Capone simply on the theory that he is dangerous and should be indicted. The tax indictment arguably could be considered ingenious prosecutorial pursuit; a phony case brought only to harass a defendant would be a fundamental and serious abuse of power. The pursuit of criminal conduct is the proper province of the prosecutor and a charge is not improper where the motive and the result are proper.

Another example is suggested by the recent Angela Davis trial (a state prosecution, not a federal case). Suppose a prosecutor decided that because a political activist presented a danger of criminal activity, he or she should be watched carefully. If this surveillance resulted in an indictment, predicated either on the kind of criminal (not political) conduct that initially made the subject appear to be dangerous or on unrelated but nonetheless criminal conduct, this, it could be argued, would be a legitimate, if political, trial. (This, according to the prosecutor, was the case in the recent Davis trial.) On the other hand, indicting a person simply for exercising constitutionally protected rights to speak, or attempting to project that protected conduct into criminal conduct (such as some form of criminal syndicalism) would result in an illegitimate political trial. A racketeer's conduct is a proper precipitant to prosecutorial investigation, and his offenses would be proper subjects of prosecution; a political leader's politics alone are neither proper precipitants nor appropriate acts to prosecute if all they have ever amounted to was constitutionally protected speech.

In addition to asking whether any prosecutor may pursue his preferred class of defendants, one must inquire also into a) the legality of the prosecutor's acts; and b) the criminality of the defendant's acts.

The question needs to be asked in "political" trials whether that conduct which directed the prosecution to conclude in the first instance that the person should be pursued was based on the judgment that the person posed a threat of criminal conduct or a political threat. It could be argued that while Capone's initial threat was one of serious criminal acts, in the case of the Berrigans the initial threat concerned their political conduct. Here, the motive of the district attorney or his investigative arm becomes relevant.

It would seem that Hoover's interest in the Berrigans began with his displeasure over their political rather than their alleged criminal activities. Later charges concerned criminal acts, but the weakness of the supportive evidence and questionable propriety of the initial prosecutorial motivation combine to make the case suspect. Unfortunately, the subjective motive of the prosecutor, while relevant, often cannot be proved.

Two further questions need to be considered in determining what is a legitimate or an illegitimate political trial. The first is the criminality of the conduct upon which the case is based. If, in fact, there is a real criminal case[12] (a murder, let us say, instead of a conspiracy or a fiery speech), the argument is strong that the motive of the prosecutor and the political ramifications of the trial are, if not irrelevant, certainly secondary.

A second consideration is how the prosecutor makes his case. Obviously, a suborned case is to be condemned, whether or not the suborned proof happens to prove a real case; under our legal system a case should not be sanctioned if proved by illegal or unconstitutional means. This conclusion is recognized in ample precedents such as those disallowing convictions based on coerced confessions, whether or not the confession was true and the crime was proven.

The prosecutor's discretion then is limited by a) the need for a legitimate criminal case upon which to predicate his indictment—including both the commission of an offense and proof that the offense was not based on constitutionally protected conduct, and

b) the requirement that his case be prosecuted according to the law.

Of course, these general principles are not empirical or formulistic equations; they cannot be applied in slide-rule fashion to show definitively whether or not a given "political" trial is legitimate. They are suggested as principles to guide the ideal prosecutor and the general public in balancing and judging a case and deciding if it is a legitimate political trial. If the Berrigan case demonstrates any one thing clearly, it is that there is a need to define and follow general principles in assessing "political" trials on something approaching a rational basis. President Nixon's disposition for clarity notwithstanding, this case proves that there is a wide and fuzzy terrain between general political goals and specific criminal cases.

Few would dispute the conclusion that the Berrigan case was not political in any sense referring to party politics, except in the most incidental and inevitable way. Furthermore, whether or not one agrees with the Nixon Justice Department's priorities, one cannot quarrel with its right to set its own policies. Moreover, Nixon's law and order philosophy and his Justice Department's crackdown on domestic radicalism was widely accepted; it was subjected to the electoral rigors of gaining popular support and being held accountable four years later. In assessing the 1968–1972 Nixon administration's Justice Department, the Berrigan case reflects disproportionately but tellingly on its character and theme; in this sense it was a highly political trial.

However, although we may conclude that Justice Department may properly have priorities, the legitimacy of their administrations should be judged by the additional criteria: the propriety of the prosecutor's motivation, the legality of the means used to prosecute, and the possibility that the criminal charges were an attempt to punish constitutionally protected acts.

Numerous legal questions were raised during the course of the Berrigan case: questions about excessive use of the grand jury and contempt power; the venerable and vexing question about the use of informers; the question of the propriety of charging broad and fluid conspiracies—so difficult to disprove and so amenable to abuse. In each of these areas, too, there are legal precedents and, in some situations, proper reasons to support the use of these techniques. They cannot then be called inherently illegal or unethical, however unwise they may be viewed and however appropriate for reformation they may be. The question of the legality of means then, like the more subjective questions about the government's motive, cannot alone resolve the issue of the case's legitimacy, although its relevance cannot be ignored. Their consideration merely compounds initial suspicions about the case.

Were the charges trumped up; and were they no more than a guileful way of discrediting or destroying dissent by persecuting dissenters? Assuming that it was, if not right, not illegal for the Justice Department to organize its efforts in a campaign against domestic radicalism; assuming also that all the aggressive weapons from the awesome arsenal of the national prosecutor's office were used according to accepted, even if questionable, legal guidelines, a critical question remains. Were the defendants tried for committing criminal acts, or was the Justice Department's machinery used to attack people who were exercising their sacred, constitutionally protected rights to wage a war of ideas—an ideological and not a criminal war—about national policy and morality?

The irregular timing and departmental politics of the case, the weakness of the government's evidence presented, the rhetorical nature of the chief offense alleged, the exotic nature of the offense that two defendants were convicted of, the reaction of the jury— all seem to support the defendants' claim that the case "was not an effort to convict them for what they had done, but an attempt to vindicate the administration for charges it could not support." Even granting the Nixon Justice Department its right to decide which cases to prosecute and how hard, this prosecution seemed a capricious and unwise use of political power.

All the facts never will be known. The jury's verdict is in; so is the public verdict, I should think, though it may be less clear and decisive. The case certainly shows the need for guiding principles to define, let alone judge, the proper role of prosecutorial discretion. No one involved in the case came out of it looking better or stronger than when it all began. The defendants—even the successful ones—were made to bear the prolonged, painful agony of trial; the government suffered a very costly public defeat.

Since the trial, J. Edgar Hoover has died, and this colossal political figure now rests in peace; a married Philip Berrigan has been released from prison by Nixon's parole board; Henry Kissinger is well and safe and secretary of state. And, the country has learned that the use of prosecutorial power is a dangerous, costly, and inefficient way to do good or to put down evil.

EPILOGUE

This chapter was written B.W., "Before Watergate"; the opportunity to re-read and re-think my analysis of political trials in light of these astounding recent revelations convinces me that my conclusions are sound.

That some of the participants in the Watergate wrongdoings were protagonists in the Berrigan case provides an ironical twist; that the whole Nixon law-and-order team has been discredited in the morality play of Watergate makes a fascinating paradox out of their first-term moral preachings and postures. One's mind is boggled considering some of the actions of these former law-enforcement officials in light of what is now known or alleged about their own specific lawlessness in office: the revelation that J. Edgar Hoover's was the voice of restraint when the White House wanted to pursue its unique notions about national security; John Ehrlichman's testimony to the Ervin Committee attempting to compare the raising of defense funds for political defendants like Angela Davis with the payments to the Watergate burglars of defense fees and hush money; John Mitchell's explanation to Senator Inouye that the difference between the notorious Liddy proposals to him and the Berrigan investigation which coincided in time was that there were "overt acts . . . as well as discussions" in the Berrigan situation.

For present purposes, at least, the most important consideration is whether the general principles suggested for evaluation of
political trials hold up or whether Watergate requires the addition
of new and qualifying lessons to this chapter. My feeling is that
the criteria recommended here can be tested by even the extraordinary events of Watergate and found to be useful and apt, and
that my conclusions are underscored by this unique piece of recent history.

Prosecutorial discretion cannot be left uncontrolled; principles
of restraint need to be applied to political cases; and constitutional principles must govern governmental action in contentious,
ideological cases even more than any others. The 1968–72 Nixon
law-and-order team, the Watergate exposé has shown, broke all
the rules.

If the Watergate disclosures direct public attention to the need
for the development of a prosecutorial morality, as the Berrigan
case did too in its own way, each of these episodes of legal-
political history will have made an important contribution beyond the fates of their own characters and issues.

NOTES

1. In the essays accompanying this one, several authors have chronicled
the rising rhetoric and accelerating course of protesting conduct on the
part of the radical church. I will not repeat the story here.

2. *The FBI and the Berrigans* (McCann & Geoghegan, 1972).

3. When John Mitchell did leave, Mardian was overlooked. Mardian
resigned and went to work for the Nixon re-election campaign.

4. *The FBI and the Berrigans*, p. 180.

5. A judgment was made on the merits. There was an indictment and
a conviction of two out of six defendants.

6. A fascinating example of the dynamics of prosecutorial discretion is
the story of the indictment of James Landis described in Victor Navasky's
Kennedy Justice (New York: Atheneum, 1971).

7. One commentator has suggested, as a way to avoid politicalization
of the Justice Department and to provide institutional restraints on prosecutorial discretion, dividing the department into two functions. He
proposes a cabinet-level legal advisor to the president, a secretary of the

Department of Law, and an independent law enforcement agency under an attorney general. See I. Silver, "The Case for Dividing Justice," *Commonweal*, July 28, 1972, p. 403.

8. For the classic exposition of the theme, see Kenneth C. Davis, *Discretionary Justice: A Preliminary Inquiry* (Baton Rouge: Louisiana State University Press, 1969).

9. Since this writing, both the Subversive Activities Control Board and the Internal Security Division have been disbanded.

10. For this reason, I predict the statute used in that case will be declared unconstitutional.

11. The predicament of the law violator who argues that he should not be punished for his violations if his motives were good differs from the classic quandary of the good German who failed to dispute or violate evil laws. Daniel Ellsberg could argue that he had a moral obligation to violate a corrupt law against disclosing classified information. He could not have made the same argument if his way of making his point about that law was to kidnap Melvin Laird. Perhaps some ultimate moral judge will excuse a criminal act on the basis not of the invalidity of the criminal law but because of the actor's overriding social justification; it is presumptuous and dangerous for us mortals to make such judgments, however, except as a personal standard for guiding our own conduct.

12. This consideration is complicated by the fact that a criminal case is on one level determined by what a jury ultimately decides, although it also involves what a prosecutor knows—which may or may not always be the same thing.

I ask you which is more dangerous, the organized criminals who perpetuate their crimes of greed, or these people who are charged here, who reject society's definition of the law and of the criminal? The organized criminal has a great deal more self-restraint. Those charged here would overthrow the structures of the society in which we live.

—Federal Prosecutor William Lynch, Harrisburg, Pennsylvania

Thus Harrisburg is an illustration of a problem but not an enlargement of it. The problem fundamentally is that the courts have not either in this country or elsewhere developed the doctrines of law that are capable of distinguishing between what are essentially political cases and those involving truly criminal behavior.

—Burke Marshall

The Issues on Trial

BURKE MARSHALL

THE VIOLATIONS OF LAW undertaken by the White House in the collection of corruption known as the Watergate affair makes it difficult to accord to a proceeding such as the Harrisburg case the normal presumption of good faith that the Department of Justice generally deserves. This is so especially because the only explanation advanced in defense of those activities, when they are defended, shows a pathological fear on the part of the administration of the kind of political dissent that the defendants at Harrisburg admittedly engaged in. It is on the basis of such a fear that the burglaries and other unlawful acts authorized by the White House are justified. The greatest of the many ironies in the establishment of such a program by an administration constantly preaching respect for law and order is that a more dangerous and vastly larger police-state effort was balked only by the bureaucratic stubbornness of Mr. Hoover and the Federal Bureau of Investigation.

The purpose of this chapter, however, is to look at the Harrisburg case as a criminal proceeding based on the conspiracy doctrine, and to judge it on the basis of the trial record, apart from the motivations of the attorney general who authorized it, and the Nixon administration's other and later efforts at repression. It may be that burglary, unlawful wiretapping, and other illegal acts were done by agents of the government in their efforts against the Harrisburg defendants, as in their efforts against

Burke Marshall was assistant attorney general in charge at the Civil Rights Division under Kennedy and Clark and is now assistant dean of Yale Law School. He is author of *Federalism and Civil Rights.*

Ellsberg. But they do not appear on the record, and it serves no purpose to speculate about that. What follows, therefore, is a view of the case as it was presented in court, as unpolluted as possible by judgments based upon the disclosures of 1973.

Already in April of 1972, it was clear that by failing to reach any verdict in the conspiracy charge contained in Count I of the Berrigan indictment, the Harrisburg jury put an end to a massive effort by the Department of Justice, of which the FBI is formally a part, to redeem its public investment in the supposed antiwar plot to kidnap Henry Kissinger. Before the trial even started, of course it had become plain that that was not what was really involved at all; whatever plot there was to be proved was to engage in a much looser kind of traditional antiwar activity, including interference in various ways with the running of the Selective Service system. But even that fell apart in the confusion of the trial itself, and the government ended up convincing the jury only that letters had been smuggled in and out of a federal prison, contrary to that institution's rules, as indeed everyone admitted from the outset. The question now remains whether there is to be gained from the trial some more general lesson about the state of our liberties, or the potential for abuse of the processes of justice, that we can apply to the future and use in judging the conduct of our public officials.

In dealing with this question, I want to put to one side the matter of the convictions of Elizabeth McAlister and Philip Berrigan on the charges of causing letters to be smuggled in and out of the United States Penitentiary at Lewisburg. Once the question whether that happened was put to the jury, it had little reason to do anything else than return verdicts against those two defendants. The evidence was that, with the assistance of Boyd Douglas, they had in fact done what they were charged with doing.

There are unquestionably very substantial legal questions as to whether McAlister and Berrigan should properly be held criminally accountable for these acts. For one thing, it is not at all clear that the prohibition against contraband contained in the criminal statute (as contrasted with the rules of the institution) applies to written material at all. It has never been administered as if it did. A more natural reconstruction of what Congress might have considered serious enough conduct to require criminal sanctions would lead one to read the statute as prohibiting the smuggling of drugs or weapons into the prison. In addition, while there is a very wide scope for prosecutorial discretion, the federal courts have set some limits on the power of the prosecutor to bring criminal charges based on a statute, or on a construction of a statute, never before thought to justify penal sanctions for the particular conduct involved. Such judicial restraint of the prosecutor is particularly appropriate where the case smacks, as does this one, of punishment of political opponents. The notion is simply one of fairness, that is, due process—that a person should not be punished for doing something no one had ever before considered to be criminal. The heavy-handed sentences imposed by Judge Herman on these counts make the use of criminal penalties as retribution against letter writing seem particularly unfair in the Berrigan case. So does the fact that, in the case of six of the seven incidents on which convictions were obtained (all three against McAlister, and three out of four against Berrigan), the actual smuggling of the documents was done by Boyd Douglas after he became an informer for the FBI, so that the acts now claimed to be criminal were known to Justice Department officials at the time they occurred, and could of course have been prevented.

Nevertheless, the convictions of McAlister and Berrigan on letter smuggling charges seem to me to raise no great or long-range issues. The points just noted were urged on Judge Herman, and are being made in more elaborate form in appellate courts. If the convictions are upheld, it will not mean that the government has become armed with a new means of political oppression, or that constitutionally protected rights have been fundamentally undermined. To be sure, some liberty is lost whenever an injustice is done, which seems to me would be true in this case, but the issues involved are not of constitutional proportions and do not in any other way acquire the dimensions that put fundamental freedoms at stake. At most, upholding the sentences would yield the Department of Justice a petty tactical victory from what is in all other respects a calamitous failure. So in looking for aspects of the Harrisburg trial that may affect the law and its administration in some lasting way, it is ironically appropriate to pass over the trial's only concrete result.

The events leading up to the indictments and trial are of a different order, involving as they do deep implications concerning the institutional controls that the Department of Justice exercises over its own actions, and the ability of the FBI, unless checked by a strong attorney general, to create cases against its enemies. The circumstances of Mr. Hoover's testimony about the supposed Berrigan plot do strongly suggest that he deliberately put the department in a position where it either had to proceed with a prosecution, almost regardless of the strength or credibility of the available evidence, or else seek his retirement. However, Mr. Hoover is dead, and the known details of the decision to prosecute, as well as its implications, are fully and carefully discussed elsewhere in these essays and in other books.

Prosecutorial discretion is, of course, inescapable. The political priorities of a national administration are reflected through its exercise by the Department of Justice. In the case of the department under the Nixon administration, there can be no escaping the fact that cases against antiwar groups have been a priority. To call this harassment and persecution of political enemies is a form of rhetorical argument against a politically established priority. I do not believe that the establishment of this priority can itself be considered an abuse of power; Francis Biddle, for example, tells in his memoirs of President Roosevelt's insistence on the disastrous prosecution in Washington of American Nazi sympathizers. It is simply one of the factors that presumably have been taken into account in some very broad and inexact way by the electorate in choosing the president, and thereby choosing between competing priorities. It is no different in principle, really, from establishing as a priority the prosecution of cases involving claimed violations of civil rights statutes, another murky and ambiguous area of criminal law where the scope of potential abuse of prosecutorial discretion is also very large. It would be very difficult even to demonstrate that the priority of surveillance and prosecution of antiwar and other protest groups, rather than other factors, has really produced its presumably desired effect of chilling that kind of activity.

In any event, the case charged a conspiracy to do acts that are in themselves unquestionably criminal, and unquestionably proper subjects of prosecution—the destruction of Selective Service records (Counts Ia and b), dynamiting United States property (Count Id and e), and kidnaping Henry Kissinger (Count If). It is true that the former charges were added in the superseding indictment, after it became clear to the lawyers who had to try the case that it was going to be very difficult to convince anyone, much less a jury confined to weighing legally admissible evidence, that the defendants really planned to kidnap Dr. Kissinger, or to blow up the heating systems of a lot of federal buildings. But the question is not whether the crime charged was properly defined as a crime. In that sense, the case stated by the indictment was quite different, for instance, from the Chicago conspiracy case or from the Smith Act prosecutions of Communist leaders, where the essence of the crimes charged was speech —inciting to riot, and advocating the violent overthrow of the government—rather than action. The statutes defining the crimes in those cases, unlike the Harrisburg case, raised substantial constitutional questions because they were directed at speech and advocacy. No such issue is presented by the Berrigan indictment on its face. The proof offered by the government, however, did give the case the smell of repression, of the use of the courts and the system of criminal justice to punish dissent, rather than any serious effort to do damage to government property, or any person. My Lynch, the trial counsel for the government, and an able, experienced courtroom lawyer, summarized his case in his opening statement to the jury in the following terms:

I mention that these defendants took very strong exception to governmental policy. Had that exception taken the traditional role of dissent, peaceful protest and working for a political change, we would not all be here. Instead they banded together, they combined, and they conspired and planned a series of illegal acts, the thrust of which was to disrupt governmental activities and to focus and exploit and, if possible, magnify news coverage of those activities.

The key word here is "illegal." The submersion of that word under all the others colored the government's case throughout. For there is nothing criminal, nothing wrong, about banding together, combining, and planning to disrupt governmental activities—that is done in all kinds of ways, including speaking, petitioning, protesting, writing, advertising, and, indeed, voting, against government policy—nor about trying to focus, exploit, or magnify what you are doing, which is at the heart of political activity. So the question of abuse of prosecutorial discretion boils down to whether the Department of Justice really believed that the defendants were seriously plotting to commit crimes, on the one hand, or whether the Department used some silly letters and conversations to punish dissent (that is, challenges of government war policies that the defendants and many others considered outrageous) that the planners intended to express in as dramatic a fashion as possible.

The jury's refusal to convict on the major charge of the indictment is not conclusive, for juries often fail to convict for one reason or another in cases that the government could not properly fail to bring to court. But it is suggestive. The government, which has great leeway in such matters, picked a forum that it considered most congenial to prosecution of antiwar groups, and framed charges that would sustain the loosest kind of finding of guilt. If the government could not convince that jury, in that area, of those charges, it is unlikely that it could have made any case stand anywhere.

On the other hand, there is no doubt that the defendants planned antiwar activities, and were participating in a movement which they thought of themselves as requiring concealment, secrecy, and even deception. There was enough evidence presented at the trial to show that it was at least not unreasonable for the government to have concluded that some of the defendants were involved in acts of vandalism that took place in Selective Service offices in Philadelphia and various locations in Delaware. To some degree that was admitted; in fact, it was their involvement in those acts that led to the outrage of the defendants and their lawyers at the superseding indictment, which appeared designed to permit convictions based solely on participation in the planning of those acts, without hard proof of the much-heralded plots to kidnap Klssinger and to blow up the federal underground heating system in Washington. Then finally there were, undeniably, the letters exchanged between Elizabeth Mc-Alister and Philip Berrigan in which she outlined "a plan for action," to "kidnap—in our terminology make a citizen's arrest of—someone like Henry Kissinger," and he said "I like the plan and am just trying to weave elements of modesty into it. Why not coordinate it with the one against capitol utilities?"

Is this enough to justify a prosecutorial decision to bring the case to court? I think not, at least not on the basic charge of a conspiracy to destroy the heating tunnels and kidnap Kissinger, which was the charge in the first indictment, and the basic public charge against the group. The government's decision must be justified, therefore, if at all, on the supporting evidence available to it, and that in turn leads to Boyd Douglas, the government informer, on whom their case depended. There was written evidence, for what it was worth, of the supposed plot to kidnap Kissinger, but the plan to blow up the tunnels was only obliquely touched on in the letters. Douglas's testimony on direct examination about the tunnels, which is presumably what he told the government when it was making its decision to prosecute, follows:

Q. In mid-May you mentioned he talked about several projects. Was there a particular project he talked about?

A. Yes. This was the destruction of the utility system in Washington, D.C.

Q. Tell us about that, what he said about that.

A. Well, he told me that he had been in this system along with another individual.

Q. What do you mean he had been in the system?

A. He had been down in the tunnel system itself with another individual. He said it was the complete utility system, and it carried conduits in the system. He said that he had been down there posing as an electrical engineer from a Robb Electrical Company. I am not sure on the Robb Electrical Company. He said he had no problem in gaining access to the tunnel, that several of the GSA people in the tunnel system raised no question to them when they were down in the tunnel.

Q. Did he tell you where he gotten access to the tunnel?

A. Yes. He said he had been down through the tunnel, through the entrance of the Forrestal building.

Q. Do you know where that is?

A. No, I do not.

Q. Continue.

A. He said that to do this action—

THE COURT: To do what?

THE WITNESS: He said that to destroy these pipes, these utility pipes in Washington itself, would be the utmost impact upon the United States Government, if they were destroyed and destroyed right. I told him at that time that I had some experience in explosives while I was in the service.

BY MR. LYNCH:

Q. Was that accurate?

A. No. I had no experience.

Q. Did you continue to talk about this project?

A. Yes, we did. He described to me—the tunnel system was approximately eight feet by ten feet wide, and that they had had no trouble walking around the tunnel itself. I asked him approximately where the conduits were located at. He didn't give me the exact location of the pipes, but that he was afraid of them erupting up through Pennsylvania Avenue or one of the main highways in Washington, D.C.

THE COURT: He said he was afraid of what?

THE WITNESS: If there were explosive devices placed, that it might possibly erupt.

THE COURT: Oh, in the street.

THE WITNESS: Yes.

He told me that it was a small tunnel system itself—a large tunnel system, and that they ran all over—well, that they ran underneath the entire streets in Washington, D.C., and that they connected all of the government buildings.

At other times during his testimony Douglas elaborated on this, giving accounts of other conversations with Berrigan, and discussions variously with Wenderoth, McLaughlin, and McAlister concerning the tunnel system. To some extent these elaborations lent credibility to the basic story, because they were concerned with details, such as the size of the tunnels, the availability of explosives, and the like. Yet none of them was specific enough to constitute proof of what most people would view as hard planning for as dangerous, ambitious, and elaborate a scheme as the jury was asked to believe existed. Further—and this was, of course, the basic weakness of the government's case— all of this evidence was what Douglas said other people told him. The sole bit of corroboration relied on by the government, which was the allegation that Berrigan and Wenderoth actually inspected the tunnels on April 1, 1970, was never proved. So this part of the case depended on believing a man with a life-long history of deception, falsehood, cheating, and betrayal, and who was indebted to boot to the FBI for his freedom and his livelihood.

The matter at issue is not whether the government made out a good enough case at trial to convince a jury, for obviously it did not. The question is whether the government abused its great powers in deciding to bring the case at all. There seems to me to be no answer to the charge that Mr. Hoover did grievously abuse his position as director of the bureau by making public accusations against Berrigan and others before any formal proceedings had been initiated or, apparently, even decided upon. Moreover, the case was inherently implausible, requiring, as it did, a total suspension of skepticism, and an affirmative belief that these defendants, including a jailed priest and a politically naive nun, could really seriously be planning to kidnap Kissinger and blow up miles of heating ducts under the city of Washington. And it did depend more on the credibility of Boyd Douglas than on any other facts.

Yet it is a most serious matter to conclude that the attorney general of the United States, with the connivance of other lawyers, including well-regarded career attorneys, violated his office by deliberately bringing criminal charges against prominent political adversaries of the administration that he knew would not stand up. On the whole, that charge is not proved. It turns on judgments about evidence and witnesses that are easier to make after the fact than before. It appears from a reading of the trial record, for example, that the government hoped to bring out from witnesses sympathetic to the defense some corroborative facts that either did not exist in the first place, or in any event could not be elicited from those witnesses. Further, the good faith of the prosecution seems to me to turn critically on one question that we have no answer to, which is why the Government failed to make any proof of the allegation that Berrigan and Wenderoth inspected the heating tunnels on April 1, 1970. This supposed event was listed as one of the overt acts in fulfillment of the alleged plot in both the original and superseding indictments. It was explicitly and unambiguously cited by Lynch, the chief prosecutor and a careful and experienced trial lawyer, in his opening statement:

The destruction of draft records was not the sole function of this group because they planned, among other things, as it were, to use one of their words, to escalate or increase their anti-government or certain policies of the government, their strong views against governmental policies, by planning the destruction of certain underground heating ducts that run in tunnels that connect certain government buildings in Washington, D.C. In fact, we expect the proof to show that Father Joseph Wenderoth and Father Philip Berrigan entered in early 1970 these underground tunnels with the intent of casing or assessing the feasibility of this particular activity.

Now this is not the kind of a statement that an experienced prosecutor will make to a jury unless he believes he can produce the goods. The goods in this case would be proof that two of the defendants actually did something in furtherance of one of the two most basic and most implausible parts of the alleged plot. Further, they would be proof independent of Boyd Douglas, concerning something that happened before Douglas had even met Berrigan or any of the defendants, and which Douglas himself could not have affected. If Lynch claimed to be able to produce proof of this kind without in fact having any way of doing so, he would not only be in violation of his professional canons of ethics, and his oath of office, but would also be deliberately laying a foundation for the destruction of his own credibility with the jury. The former would be inconsistent with Lynch's entire career in the Department of Justice, under more than one administration, and the latter with his ability and experience, wholly apart from his ethics. So it appears that he must have had evidence that failed him, or that he decided to withhold it for some tactical reason; but not that the government was proceeding solely on the basis of Douglas's story, untested by any objective facts. If this is so, the decision to prosecute, while highly questionable and certainly arguably wrong, cannot be termed a plain abuse of power.

What then of the manner in which the government framed and attempted to prove its case? The public concern in this area centers on two aspects of the proceeding: First, the crime charged was a conspiracy, a plot, an agreement, talk about action without either of the principal acts that were part of the alleged plan—the destruction of the tunnels or the Kissinger kidnaping—ever being brought remotely close to realization. Second, the government based its case on the testimony of an informer, a turncoat who had participated in the plot as a double agent, a rather typical informer, with an extensive criminal record, a history of lying, cheating, and deceit, paid to spy on a radical church group which believed him to be their friend and convert, a man who made possible by his own acts as an informer six of the seven instances of letter smuggling of which Berrigan and McAlister were convicted.

The latter of these factors involves the government in a very sordid and dirty business, and the former smacks of political persecution. Both accordingly are properly matters of public concern. But both have a long history and are deeply rooted in the traditions of law enforcement.

CONSPIRACY INDICTMENTS

First, then, the conspiracy doctrine goes back for some centuries into the origins of our legal system, perhaps to the thirteenth or at least the fourteenth centuries. Professor Thomas Emerson of Yale has said that the doctrine "has been consistently and frequently used against emerging groups who are seeking a higher and more powerful status in society," and that is so. The principal political trials in this country have been conspiracy trials—the sedition case against domestic Nazis during World War II; all of the Smith Act cases against domestic Communist leaders, including the famous trial against Eugene Dennis and others in the late 1940s; the Chicago trial following the 1968 Democratic Convention in that city, and the similar trial in Seattle during 1970; the Black Panther trial in New York City; and the Harrisburg case itself. These cases all proved basically disastrous for the prosecution and for the public perception of justice; valid convictions were obtained only in the *Dennis* case, and those very debatable constitutionally, and all the trials except the one in Harrisburg were marked by disorder, acrimony, and a lack of dignity of process. Professor Emerson points out in addition that the law of conspiracy was used for many years, starting with a British case against journeyman tailors in 1721, against embryonic labor organizations. It has also served as the prosecutorial vehicle against groups with baser motivations, notably organized crime and labor racketeers, and some of the most far-reaching rules favoring the prosecution have been developed in antitrust cases against highly regarded business interests, particularly in tobacco and oil. The classic complaint against this loose form of prosecution is that of Justice Robert Jackson, a former attorney general, in a Mann Act case called *Krulewitch* v. *United States,* 336 U.S. 440 at pages 445–48 (1949) (footnotes omitted):

This case illustrates a present drift in the federal law of conspiracy which warrants some further comment because it is characteristic of the long evolution of that elastic, sprawling and pervasive offense. Its history exemplifies the "tendency of a principle to expand itself to the limit of its logic." The unavailing protest of courts against the growing habit to indict for conspiracy in lieu of prosecuting for the substantive offense itself, or in addition thereto, suggests that loose practice as to this offense constitutes a serious threat to fairness in our administration of justice.

The modern crime of conspiracy is so vague that it almost defies definition. Despite certain elementary and essential elements, it also, chameleon-like, takes on a special coloration from each of the many independent offenses on which it may be overlaid. It is always "predominantly mental in composition" because it consists primarily of a meeting of minds and an intent.

The crime comes down to us wrapped in vague but unpleasant connotations. It sounds historical undertones of treachery, secret plotting and violence on a scale that menaces social stability and the security of the state itself. "Privy conspiracy" ranks with sedition and rebellion in the Litany's prayer for deliverance. Conspiratorial movements do indeed lie back of the political assassination, the *coup d'état,* the *putsch,* the revolution, and seizures of power in modern times, as they have in all history.

The trouble is that the crime is in the agreement, and that no illegal act need take place—Henry Kissinger need not be kidnaped, and the heating ducts need never be disturbed. People whose use of words is uncorrupted by training often take the

word "agreement" to mean in this connection what it usually
means, that is, a formal understanding, contract, or treaty, but
this is not so. The cases say, and therefore the judge instructs the
jury, that the agreement can be implied from the most casual of
circumstances, without any meeting of the conspirators, or even
necessarily communication among all of them. It is true that
conspiracy doctrine normally requires that an overt act be taken
in furtherance of the conspiracy, that some step have been made
that moves the venture ahead. Yet this also turns out to be no real
hurdle at all, for the overt act shown may be a completely lawful,
indeed trivial, event. Thus it is that the Harrisburg superseding
indictment alleged thirty-five overt acts, including such as the
claim that on May 4, 1970, Scoblick was driven to Fourth and G
Streets, NE, in Washington, where he remained for a while in the
back of a locked truck; that on June 19, 1970, McLaughlin made
a telephone call to Lewisburg, Pennsylvania; that on August 10,
1970, Scoblick traveled to Lewisburg; and that on August 17,
1970, McAlister, co-conspirators Davidon and Egan, and Paul
Mayer (who is not otherwise identified in the indictment) traveled to Connecticut.

The advantage to the prosecution of charging a group of
people in any way connected with each other with so loose a
crime is increased by the fact that the whole case can be per-
meated with what would normally be considered hearsay statements, untested by cross-examination of the person making them.
This comes about by reason of a kind of an agency theory that
once persons are shown to be in a conspiracy with each other,
each is responsible for anything any other one says or does.
There is logically an order of proof implicit in this, that the
conspiracy should be proved first before the statements of conspirator A can be admitted as evidence against conspirator B. But
this is avoided by admitting everything "subject to connection"
by some other evidence that a conspiracy has been shown at least
prima facie to exist, and the jury is expected to unravel it all at
the end of the trial. We are indebted to Justice Jackson again for
a description of how this all really looks (336 U.S. at page 453):

When the trial starts, the accused feels the full impact of the conspiracy strategy. Strictly, the prosecution should first establish *prima
facie* the conspiracy and identify the conspirators, after which evidence of acts and declarations of each in the course of its execution
are admissible against all. But the order of proof of so sprawling a
charge is difficult for a judge to control. As a practical matter, the
accused often is confronted with a hodgepodge of acts and statements
by others which he may never have authorized or intended or even
known about, but which help to persuade the jury of existence of the
conspiracy itself. In other words, a conspiracy often is proved by
evidence that is admissible only upon assumption that conspiracy
existed. The naive assumption that prejudicial effects can be overcome by instructions to the jury, . . . all practicing lawyers know
to be unmitigated fiction.

The Harrisburg trial broke no new ground in any of this. It
was clear from their questions that the jury was highly confused
by the court's charge on the law of conspiracy, but it would be
remarkable if the jury were not so confused, and its refusal to
convict on the conspiracy count in Harrisburg as well as the
Chicago case and the New York Black Panther case suggests that
juries are more careful and fairer in such cases than the appellate
courts that announce the legal doctrine. The only real argument
over conspiracy doctrine at the trial was whether the government
should be allowed to expand its list of co-conspirators after the
indictment was returned, by its answers to a bill of particulars. It
was to the advantage of the government to do so in order to make
use of the doctrine just referred to that the statements of one co-
conspirator can be used as evidence not only against him, as in
the usual case, but also against the other alleged conspirators,
even when they had no knowledge of the statements and, of
course, no opportunity to cross-examine or confront the person
who made them. The court ruled in favor of the government on
this point, but it made no significant difference at the trial. The
other points that might have been raised on an appeal probably
would have centered on questions of variance, that is whether the
government had proved the conspiracy alleged (to kidnap Kis-

singer and blow up the heating tunnels) or only some lesser plot (for example, to vandalize Selective Service offices), but those questions also were mooted by the verdict.

Thus Harrisburg is an illustration of a problem, but not an enlargement of it. The problem fundamentally is that the courts have not, either in this country or elsewhere, developed doctrines of criminal law that are capable of distinguishing between what are essentially political cases and those involving truly criminal behavior. The application of the conspiracy doctrine to the Harrisburg defendants is offensive, as it was also to an even greater degree in the Communist trials under the Smith Act, because evidence of their antiwar activities, meetings, and planning was permitted to be introduced as evidence of a plot, and once that was done, any statement by any member of the group, however unreliable otherwise, could be taken as evidence against all the others. With Boyd Douglas thrown into the picture, this meant that anything he testified that any of the claimed conspirators said at any time became admissible against all of them, including the conversations he claimed to have had with Berrigan about the heating ducts. This raises issues and concerns about the freedom of political expression which would not occur to anyone were the same rules of evidence and substantive law being applied against organized crime leaders, or corporate presidents, who planned but did not actually participate in heroin traffic or in price fixing.

INFORMERS

The same difficulty, it seems to me, lies at the heart of the discomfort we feel at the use of Boyd Douglas as an informer against these defendants. The traditional answer by law enforcement officials to objections to the use of informers, as well as wiretapping, bugging, and other forms of eavesdropping, is that it may be a dirty business, but so is crime a dirty business, and the job of law enforcement bodies is to prevent and punish crime. The counteranswer is that this may be true, but political activity, including activity directed against government programs and a national war, is not a dirty business. It is peculiarly in need of protection, not prosecution, and vital to a system of freedom. The problem is in making the distinction.

An illustration of this difficulty took place in 1964 in Mississippi. In that year the Department of Justice received almost daily reports of violent intimidation of Blacks and civil rights workers—bombings, shootings, beatings, church burnings, cross burnings, and the like—so widespread in scope that it seemed inescapably the consequence of group activity, probably of some chapters of the Ku Klux Klan. The situation grew so bad that in the late spring Attorney General Kennedy wrote President Johnson a memorandum detailing a number of incidents and recommending strongly increased federal law-enforcement efforts. Allen Dulles was sent to Mississippi as a personal representative of the president. When he returned, he recommended the immediate establishment of a large FBI field office in Jackson, as had the attorney general. While this was a matter of administration of the bureau that Mr. Hoover would normally consider outside interference, he was maneuvered by the president not only into opening a new office, but going to Jackson personally to do so. When the three civil rights workers, Schwerner, Chaney, and Andy Goodman, were murdered in Neshoba County in late June, the bureau was able to break the case. During the next eighteen months or so, it was able also effectively to break the Klan.

How was this done? It was done by the extensive use of men like Boyd Douglas, by bribery, by payments to informers, by whatever eavesdropping was then permitted under the bureau's rules, by the sowing of suspicion among Klan members so that none knew who was an informer and who was not, by infiltration and deception, and in at least one incident by the participation of a bureau informer in the planning and attempted execution of a murder.

It did not appear to those involved at the time, and it does not appear to me now, that the criminal conspiracy of violence that existed in the State of Mississippi then could have been handled by less drastic measures. The nation was in no mood, and should not have been ready, to tolerate more violence and killings directed against Black people seeking only to exercise their rights, and the whites from the North who were trying to help. If the violence had not been stopped by some means, an eventual answer would have had to be found in the direct use of troops, or some substitute federal force, with all the loss of civil liberties and local authority that that implies.

It is not as easy as it may seem to say that the use of informers such as Boyd Douglas is justified in that situation, because of the violence, but not in the surveillance of antiwar groups, because that is essentially political activity. The distinction is not so clear on either side. The Klan has a tradition of violence, but has adopted from time to time the rhetoric of peaceful protest. In addition, the Klan was simply at the extreme of a political position, deeply held by many whites of all classes in Mississippi, that supported the caste system and the legal exploitation and subjugation of Blacks. Investigation of the Klans could thus over any protracted period of time move inexorably towards investigation and infiltration of other white supremacy groups, including White Citizens' Councils or the Independence Party. On the other side, the antiwar group involved in the Harrisburg trial included persons who, although schooled in nonviolent civil disobedience, by their own admission did not believe that the antiwar movement should confine itself to constitutionally protected methods of protest or efforts at persuasion, but should instead engage also in unlawful acts, at least including trespass and destruction of government property in Selective Service offices, in order to dramatize their feelings.

Professor Emerson and some other distinguished scholars and writers on the system of freedom believe that it is possible to articulate standards to be applied by courts and law enforcement bodies that would permit the use of informers in the situation in Mississippi I have described, but forbid their use against groups such as the informal one involved in the Harrisburg case. There are two presently existing legal obstacles to doing so, apart from the difficulty of formulating the standards themselves. One is that the law at the present is that the use of informers does not constitute a search or seizure within the meaning of the Fourth Amendment, which is at least the most readily available constitutional provision by which to control the use of this form of eavesdropping. The other is that there would then have to be developed some doctrine whereby warrants or other forms of advance permission for the use of informers would be granted in cases like the Mississippi one and not in cases like that in Harrisburg. The experience under the wiretap legislation does not suggest that courts are likely to exercise this kind of control over the executive. Whatever else can be said for these proposals, therefore, it seems certain that their enactment is not a clear or present possibility, and that in the meantime we will have to rely on the wisdom of juries, the good faith and discretion of prosecutor and investigative agencies, and the effectiveness of the political process in this country.

This generation is the first in which the danger is total and the cry of despair grows from the fear of the impending death of all mankind. . . . Who could miss the knowledge that in the generation of the H-bomb, the old ideas of God had become inadequate to human liberation and human survival?

—Arthur Waskow

The radical man—or at least the radical priest—may be working for "the new man in the new society." But the man of politics cannot wait for that far-off blessed coming. He must plan for the old man in the old society. . . . There has not yet been a real revolution. And will not be.

—Michael Novak

The Pursuit of Legitimacy

JOHN C. RAINES

Strength and resolution command respect . . . but weakness and
naive sentimentality breed contempt.
—Richard M. Nixon, campaign speech, 1972

IT SEEMS ASTONISHING that the case was ever brought. With the
two principal personalities both in jail, why not let "the Berrigans" pass benignly into public forgetfulness? One reason advanced is FBI Director Hoover, who supposedly put the Justice
Department in a bind. With a passion for revenge against those
like Father Daniel Berrigan who made the Bureau into a bit of a
joke by a successful sojourn in the underground, Hoover took it
upon himself to announce "a grand conspiracy" and subsequently had to be rescued.

Plausible enough. Indeed, as far as it goes surely true. But it
doesn't go far enough: either to explain why the Berrigans and
the radical Catholic left became such a celebrated affair to begin
with, or why the Mitchell Justice Department didn't let the
Hoover charges die the death of a thousand-time-reiterated "continuing investigation." I think it is perfectly clear that the Nixon
administration thought it had caught its critics in a major public
relations snaffoo, and welcomed the opportunity to morally discredit those who criticized the morality of its war in Vietnam.
Special prosecutor William Lynch clearly had something like this
in mind in arguing for maximum bail. "I ask you which is more
dangerous," he posed to the judge, "the organized criminals who

John Raines teaches religion at Temple University. He is author of
Attack on Privacy and editor (with Tom Dean) of *Marxism and Radical
Religion*. He has been active in the civil rights and peace movements.

perpetrate their crimes of greed, or these people who are charged here, who reject society's definition of the law and of the criminal?" He answered without hesitation: "The organized criminal has a great deal more self-restraint. Those charged here would overthrow the structures of the society in which we live."

To understand the Harrisburg trial as something more than an isolated and rather bizarre event, to see its connection to more recent revelations like Watergate, the IT&T merger scandal, and the Ellsberg trial it is necessary to place these examples of judicial practice in the wider context of our cultural ethos. That ethos is best understood in terms of liberal individualism's idea of society as a marketplace of contending powers, the push and shove of rival interest groups. My thesis is this: that the central "explanations" about man and society, which up to now have provided our style of culture with its fundamental justifications are starting to unravel, a fact illustrated in the Harrisburg case in two ways. (1) The first has to do with the type of religion and morality represented by the defendants, which has been called naive. Politically, that seems fair enough. Although those who take that position have not yet explained why the furor arose in the first place, or why once started the administration couldn't leave it alone. If part of politics is to capture public attention, then the Berrigans were certainly political in that sense. Be that as it may, it is the religion and morality of the defendants, not their politics, that I want to examine. For it was a very different kind of Catholicism operating at Harrisburg from that expressed by American Catholicism's most astute liberal spokesman, Fr. John Courtney Murray. "The 'adult' State," he said, and by this I suppose he meant America, "conscious of the autonomy proper to its adulthood [is] not merely impatient of any political tutelage exercised from without by the Church, but rightfully free from such external tutelage because the means for its self-direction to right spiritual and moral ends exists within the political order itself—I mean the whole range of democratic institutions."[1]

Father Murray announces an era of democratic consensus, of religious toleration, and noninterference with the state. It parallels his good friend Reinhold Niebuhr's conclusion about the same time (early fifties) that America had achieved "a tolerable measure of justice" and so could turn its energies abroad. You can see how comforting all this would be to those who had already made it in America!

Father Murray and Professor Niebuhr spoke for a wider constituency of those who have come to be called Christian realists. It was a perspective upon reality which gained psychic poise by cultivating a certain tragic sensibility. In retrospect this was perhaps less of a religious transcending of the ruling liberal-individualist consensus than its transcendental consolation, and so its earthly consolidation. That argument will be presented later.

Now all this is in stark contrast to the fundamental religious and moral perceptions of the radical Catholic left and the wager it makes about "how things really are" and what we need to do. With a less tragic sense of man's moral and rational capacities, and a natural law heritage which speaks normatively to the state about distributive justice, the defendants at Harrisburg posed a religious and moral alternative to the liberal-realist establishment, and so raised questions as to its legitimacy.

(2) The second place where the ruling consensus showed strain was in the thinly disguised use of prosecutorial power to stifle political dissent. All this of course went quite beyond the "gentleman's rules" of proper judicial discretion beloved (quite properly) by legal scholars. But as Victor Navasky made clear in his *Kennedy Justice*, it went not much further beyond these rules than the legal snares devised by the get-Hoffa squad of the previous administration.

Indeed, and here is the point, under the legitimating set of social explanations called Liberal-individualism, the imposition of self-restraint, of "things that just aren't done," is given no theoretically necessary place to stand. It is constantly subject to being overwhelmed by an arrogance of power. Why? because the liberal power-marketplace view of social reality is just that, a marketplace, where each side is to press its advantage until restrained by the power of the other. It is a kind of automatic morality or post-morality which undermines internal demands for moral restraint that the self brings upon itself. It represents a cynicism concerning man's moral possibilities that looks instead to marketplace mechanisms to adjudicate interest biases. It is a cynicism, however, which views itself as a praiseworthy moral modesty. The Harrisburg case reveals the limits of this provisional sophistication. Man's public sense of moral seriousness, without which he grows indifferent of his consequences, can be sustained only by roots that reach into different ground. In the Harrisburg people this appeared as a kind of Catholic fundamentalism—like Thomas Merton, medieval.

This, then, is the case I want to argue. What was going on at Harrisburg can be viewed as the conflict of rival legitimacies, the foundering of liberal realism as a system of social explanation. We will examine these issues in reverse order, treating first the question of "liberalism and coercion" and then its "heavenly justifications." Finally, we shall return to what the Harrisburg defendants seemed to be groping for: "a new sense of commonweal."

LIBERALISM AND COERCION

For centuries the scepter and the orb were the companion symbols of political legitimacy in the West. They pointed to a dual source of political authority: (1) a preponderance of coercive force, and (2) the certification of religious and moral correctness. The power side of this equation seems simple enough to understand. It is what Hobbes saw as the essence of rule: the power of Leviathan in face of its citizenry to "overawe them all," and so unite and govern them. All rule, and therefore also legitimate rule, has in part to do with the ability to coerce obedience. Politics is at least the question of who rules whom— thus, the scepter.

But what about the orb? Does it refer to anything real in modern secular states? Sociologist Karl Mannheim certainly thinks so. "We belong to a group," he says, "not only because we are born into it, not merely because we profess to belong to it, nor finally because we give it our loyalty and allegiance, but primarily because we see the world and certain things in the world the way it does (i.e., in terms of the meanings of the group in question)."[2] That a state becomes *our state* has less to do with power than with our performance of its common meanings by which we "make sense" of the time we spend there. Political scientist John Scharr has analyzed the significance of this. "When leaders and followers interact on levels [of] mutual, subjective comprehension and sharing of meaning, then we say that there exists humanly significant leadership."[3] Legitimacy has to do with this co-performance of values between the leaders and the led. It is this shared world of public meanings that wins us out of our private preoccupations and presents the public world as a place worthy of our energy and attention. Put simply, although the scepter can coerce obedience, without the orb it cannot fuel the common life, it cannot lead.

Liberalism and legitimacy. All this seems obvious enough that we begin to wonder how so many social scientists could have come to interpret politics as simply a marketplace of contending powers. We wonder at this onesidedness, that is, until it dawns upon us that precisely this power-marketplace definition of society reflects our established public philosophy, the meanings and values we co-perform in our common life. Social scientists believe they have exhausted the topic of politics when they have analyzed the marketplace of interests and power because they are *liberal* social scientists. As Michael Walzer has pointed out, "Liberal society is conceived as a voluntary association of private men, egoists and families of egoists, a world not of friends and comrades but of strangers."[4]

It is in this light that President Nixon's notion of respect— "strength and resolution command respect but weakness and naive sentimentality breed contempt"—begins to reveal its wider cultural significance. His emphasis upon coercive power, upon "winning," as the real substance of public respect is not idiosyncratic. It is less biographical than historical and cultural. What the president is giving voice to, as Garry Wills has argued convincingly, is the liberal individualist worldview with its power-interest definition of the human situation. And it is this liberal realism which in large measure defines and orders the public space of contemporary America. Respect in marketplace competition is what is respectable in our society. "Proving oneself in the free arena of competition is the test of manhood, truth, and political wisdom . . . [for] there is no honor but in the Wonderland race we must all run, all trying to win."[5]

It is interesting to note that liberalism arose as a kind of moral modesty, or better yet, as what in retrospect appears a curious combination of excessive pessimism and excessive optimism. We see this in Adam Smith's famous defense of the free market. "The statesman," he pointed out,

who should attempt to direct private people in what manner they ought to employ their capitals, would not only load himself with a most unnecessary attention, but would assume an authority which could . . . nowhere be so dangerous as in the hands of a man who had folly and presumption enough to fancy himself fit to exercise it.

No man is good enough to be his brother's keeper. But happily there is an alternative. For even though the entrepreneur, "intends only his own gain . . . he is . . . led by an invisible hand to promote an end which was not part of his intention. . . . By pursuing his own interest he frequently promotes that of the society more effectively than when he really intends to promote it."[6]

Liberalism both overstates the problem
and understates its remedy.

On the one side we are to believe that man is never so much moved as when he is moved by the interests of his selfishness—a shallow and superficial view of man that cannot account for most of our everyday activity. On the other, we are to trust in the "invisible hand" of the market as a kind of secularized divine providence operating behind the scenes to bring man's selfish purposes to good.

This is liberal individualism's wager: since man cannot be trusted, it is the power-interest marketplace and its processes of competition and compromise that are the best foundation of society. It is, as Theodore Lowi has seen, a kind of "automatic society." "There is therefore no substance. Neither is there procedure. There is only process."[7] And the process is the process of push and shove. More precisely, it is push until someone else successfully shoves back. It is, in short, *the pursuit of winning*. For each side is responsible only to pursue its own interests vigorously. The marketplace mechanism takes care of balancing ambitions into eventual social benefit. Beyond this there is nothing of principle involved, nothing normative, no implicit limits. It encourages, as you can see, a catastrophic loss of the sense of "the inappropriate," of *self-restraint* as differentiated from marketplace countervailing power.

Unfettered ambition is marvelously transformed not just into an instrument of the common good but into its sole foundation. But the alchemy doesn't work. The unintended, yet logically implicit, consequence of all this is that the scepter becomes the criteria of the orb, that the estimate of "what is legitimate" as public behavior is reduced to the strategies and counterstrategies of winning. Witness:

SENATOR BAKER: The White House horrors and the breakin to the Watergate on June 17, all of those things were inferior in importance to the ultimate re-election of the President?

FORMER ATTORNEY GENERAL JOHN MITCHELL: I had no doubt about it at that time and I have no doubt about it now.[8]

It is this moral poverty of liberalism, its inability to maintain an inner sense of limits, of "the impermissible," that links the events of Watergate and Harrisburg, of the IT&T merger scandal and the Vesco investment case into a common story. And that is the story of the lonely pursuit of respect, the story of Richard Nixon, who as Vice President was never invited into the private quarters of the White House, marrying his daughter to Ike's only grandson, the story of "making it" and so gaining recognition. It is the story of winning and of "winner's justice" where the decision to prosecute is transformed from a necessary part of judicial discretion into an active instrument of seeking political or pecuniary advantage.

This makes the Harrisburg case into something more than an isolated curiosity. That the case was brought at all reflects the deep story of our liberal-individualist culture. It is, moreover, this same ethos of unfettered ambition which explains the increasing frustrations that faced civil dissent in the late sixties and led finally to the Harrisburg defendants' exotic conversations.

The image of the winner

It was, after all, a very particular kind of foolishness—this talk about kidnaping Henry Kissinger. The preposterousness of cloistering the president's chief foreign policy adviser with well-known scholars and public figures who would then grill the truth from him is at least a preposterousness on the side of democracy. For democracy depends upon the consent of an informed citizenry, and an informed citizenry depends upon truth telling between the leaders and those they seek to lead.

Hannah Arendt has reflected upon the significance of the *Pentagon* Papers in this regard.[9] The central fact illustrated there she interprets as the startling defactualization of the political realm. Questions of face, of reputation, the language of "scenarios" and "audiences" preoccupy the talk of the decision-makers. This thinning out of the facticity of public life deprives the citizen of the political means to *be* a citizen. He is left as a kind of client, a consumer, someone to be sold. And this mightily undercuts the ground upon which traditional civil protest sought to establish its case.

The attempt to raise ignored or minority positions into serious public debate by dramatic means of public expression gets trivialized in the counterstrategies of image manipulation. There's simply no serious dialogue partner on the other end, only an advertising specialist. And when image maintenance replaces citizen consent, it is government that invites the morally serious citizen into desperate and sometimes foolish conjectures about how to get back on the agenda of serious public concern.

Democracy, however, depends upon more than truth telling. It depends upon a vitality of voluntary associations to keep political loyalties complex, less than total, and thus free. Here again the lessons of Harrisburg bear upon our wider cultural ethos. Interest-group liberalism cannot understand subsidiary associations as communities of loyalty. It can view them only as conglomerates of selfishnesses, temporary interest alliances, to be dealt with not with honor but as marketplace rivals to be overwhelmed. Winning is jealous; it's suspicious of undefeated loyalties—in Watergate, of an opposing political party; at Harrisburg, of a community largely of priests and nuns.

This attack upon community is reflected in the administration's use of the Harrisburg grand jury. Until recently the investigatory grand jury, with its awesome power of subpoena and immunity, has been associated in the public mind with organized crime. It has been viewed as an instrument for undoing that comradeship of silence which preserves the conspiracy that organizes crime. Ironically, this conspiracy is a contractual association not so different from the associations of private benefit that liberal individualism conceives of as fueling the wider society, except that it pursues the end of the "contract of interest" by illegal means.

In each case, individuals are associated for the purpose of pursuing private advantage. Bringing to bear, therefore, the pressure of legal jeopardy upon individual members as a means of breaking open the comradeship of silence and so exposing it to law-enforcement proceedings would seem simply to raise the stakes in the same game of self-interest already accepted by the associated members. But what happens when these same legal instruments are used on an association whose binding ties are not self-interest but common value allegiance? Such was the case with Sr. Jogues Egan at Harrisburg or the Florida grand jury on the

Viet Nam Veterans Against the War. Now the immunity power is brought to bear upon a comradeship of loyalty, not a contract of private interests. It seeks to substitute the game of calculating individual advantage and disadvantage into a very different game. It gets into the business of coercing conscience, undermining its integrity by inducing betrayal of comrades, attacking the substance of community.

Here law becomes a potent weapon against associational life and is in danger of undermining democracy. For it is these associations of common loyalty, especially when they depart from purely personal concerns to enter with seriousness into matters of public affairs, that create distance between the self and the general social system and so make room for citizen consent. Administrators of justice who desire that the justice they administer also be of service to democracy, will use these potent weapons only with the greatest discretion, carefully drawing the line of "crime" to protect the vitality of political dissent and opposition, rigorously avoiding any "fishing expeditions" that expose to legal jeopardy parties innocent of any suspected crime but who are loyal to a wider comradeship of shared values with those directly suspected. The lessons from Harrisburg with Sr. Jogues Egan and from the Camden Twenty-eight grand jury which sent Mr. and Mrs. Grumbles to jail for eighteen months because of their refusal to testify—although the prosecutors knew them to be innocent of any direct involvement—indicates that we have a long way to go on this matter.

If we turn to the issue of informers, these questions concerning the use of law enforcement instruments to attack community become even more graphic. The effectiveness of an informer depends upon loyalty: its building up and its sudden betrayal. Far more than wire tap or other forms of technological surveillance, informers use the very stuff of community to undermine, expose, and so destroy community. Consequently, the acquiring and placement of an informer and the determination of the permissible bounds of his activity, require constant and rigorously circumscribed supervision. But at present, although court proceedings to "show probable cause" are now required in all but foreign security cases for the placement of wire taps, no formal proceedings at all are mandated for the acquisition, placement, and use of informers.

How casual and massive is the present use of informers is strikingly illustrated in the Media FBI files.[10] A bureau notification from the office of the director on November 4, 1970 instructs "all" local FBI officers to infiltrate and report upon "*all* Black Student Unions" in their respective areas. A portion of that chilling memo reads as follows.

Each office submit by airtel, to reach Bureau by 12/4/70, a list of BSU's and similar groups by name and school which are or will be subjects of preliminary inquiries. This program will include junior colleges and two-year colleges as well as four-year colleges. In connection with this program there is a need for increased source coverage, and we must develop a network of discreet quality sources in a position to furnish required information.

Surely the potential damage of informer use upon the targeted community, and to the wider climate of public freedom, calls for a much more stringently drawn set of regulations. This seems especially clear given the notorious history of informers becoming *agents provocateur* in order to keep themselves in business. This is illustrated not only in the Harrisburg case, but in the Florida case on the Viet Nam Veterans Against the War, the Tommy-the-traveler Hobart College students' trial, the Camden Twenty-eight trial, and in innumerable drug cases. Indeed, this whole area is so out-of-control that it requires the immediate attention of both Congress and the courts.

In a word, as regards both immunity use and the placement of informers, the central issue is the difference between the politics of democratic rule and the politics of marketplace conquest and control. "Winner's justice" not only poorly serves, it gravely threatens democracy. "Strength and resolution" deserve "respect" only in so far as they are accompanied by a firm sense of self-restraint and fair play. But liberalism's power-interest view of society does not know and cannot teach us this.

Watergate, Harrisburg, the attempt to bribe the judge at the Ellsberg trial, terrorist drug raids, political "dirty tricks" that subvert the electoral process, strong-arming political contributions from airlines or political caution from television networks, behind-the-scenes boondoggle profits for big grain corporations while the American housewife picks up the tab for the Russian wheat deal—have we become so inured to the shenanigans of winning that we no longer become angry at this shameless use of power? If so, then the preservation of civilized society has been poorly served by our established view of social reality.

HEAVENLY JUSTIFICATIONS

Harrisburg was about a trial, the use and misuse of law. It was also about a religious and moral confrontation that brought into question the legitimacy of the liberal-realist consensus at deeper level.

Part of the task of a society in seeking to legitimate itself is the provision of persuasive consolation. For there is an *inevitable quality of overcoming* in the task of establishing legitimacy: overcoming the enervating sense of how unfairly we are in fact treated not only by each other but by fate, overcoming our loss of confidence in the reasonableness and significance of our public lives. In the case of liberal individualism, we have seen that Adam Smith argued for his "hidden hand" not simply because he thought it was there, but because he found in the idea solace for what he believed were the inevitable egoistic limits on human virtue. We should note in this regard that certain recent religious thinkers did not so fundamentally transcend this liberal imagination as they believed. Reinhold Niebuhr remains the most sophisticated of these religious realists. He also had great influence on secular intellectuals. Since in one way or another he spoke for many, we can use his theory as our single illustration.

Niebuhr began where Adam Smith did, with the ineluctable selfishness of man, but he found Smith's consolation (the hidden hand) naive, and thus incapable of supplying the sense of confi-

dence necessary to fund man's vital public life. Niebuhr set about
the task of its religious reconstruction and so, more than he knew,
supplied liberal society with a "heavenly justification." How so?

For Niebuhr, man stands "at the juncture of nature and spirit;
and is involved in both freedom and necessity."[11] This fundamental instability gives rise to an anxiety which is the precondi-
tion of the self's inordinate self-estimate. Sin displays itself as an
insatiable egoisim and will to power. It is inextricably mixed with
man. This human "nature" then sets the boundaries on what can
reasonably be hoped for in society. Both cynicism and utopian-
ism misread the indeterminate possibilities of man's grandeur
and misery. What is required instead is a worldly-wise faith that
is able to trust the ultimate power of God to bring to good what
remains in man's hands at best ambiguous; "a faith," as Niebuhr
says, "which understands the fragmentary and broken character
of all historic achievements and yet has confidence in their
meaning because it knows their completion to be in the hands of a
Divine Power, whose resources are greater than those of men, and
whose suffering love can overcome the corruptions of man's
achievements, without negating the significance of our striv-
ing."[12] History remains forever a place that points beyond itself
. . . to the hidden purposes of God and to an eternal homeland
for forgiven and reconciled selves. For Niebuhr, it is in this sense
that life can be seen to make sense.

This understanding of evil and its final overcoming deeply
conditions the realist's view of politics. Following from this view
of the self, society is interpreted primarily as a scene of competing individual and group vitalities—as distinguished, for example, from Saint Thomas Aquinas, who looked upon society as
the cradle of human language and thus of human rationality. It is
a marketplace of prides, powers, and interests in various modes of
conflict and negotiation. Which is to say that the good society too
remains but an arena of private interests and vitalities, only
socially managed into a relative equilibrium. The moral task
becomes to increase relative justice by increasing through organization and alliances the power of various marginal groups and

consequently their bargaining position in the social marketplace.

Meanwhile, and here is the consolation, the perspective of divine completion supplies that psychic poise to carry on the indeterminate task of the endless arena, reminding us of a final homeland in what remains a kind of exile—a society, as Walzer said, of egoists and families of egoists, not comrades of a common civilization but at best fellow teammates suspiciously eyeing the market "to get our fair share." All of which is to say that religious realism does not so much treanscend liberal individualism as reflect it in a transcendental manner. It is liberalism's "heavenly completion," its halo of confidence and vitality.

Now I want to pose three criticisms to this point of view each of which moves us in the direction of a more traditionally Catholic reading of society. For it is my contention that this more classical and medieval perspective upon society—the heritage of the Harrisburg defendants—provides greater critical insight upon our times than that sophisticated realism which fuels the ruling consensus.

First, the realism of establishment realism is insufficient because it cannot in fact explain society but begins its explanations only after already taking society for granted. Any social explanation which starts with the marketplace metaphor must assume a whole prior level of social reality which we can call *the common virtues of everyday life*. I have in mind the necessary assumption of relative dependability in each others' word and work that allows us to carry on the tasks of the common life without constantly tripping over our suspicion of one another. Or again, there is that everyday virtue, so inordinately practiced most of the time, of giving the other guy the benefit of a doubt, that graciousness of spirit which fuels the common life even as it exposes it to the unscrupulous. Or there is the astonishing generosity of everyday living, with its manifold gestures of uncoerced and unrewarded helpfulness without which a society grows narrow, envious, and endlessly calculating, coming at last to a kind of standstill. In short, I refer to the whole thickness of the everyday world, our common exposure before life and consequent reliance upon one another. This is the fundamental dimension of man's ordering of his existence, and to it the marketplace negotiations of interest and power remain second-level realities—able to disrupt but not able to create or survive without. Put simply, the power-interest model of society takes society for granted because it is incapable of finding an interpretive place for the realities of community and of the common good that lie at the base of man's collective existence.

Second, American interest-group pluralism took for granted that which in the latter half of the twentieth century needs increasingly to become a matter of conscious human planning and priority: namely, the care and nurture of the *shared public realm* as a common life-space of mutual benefits and threatened disasters. The decay of the central service facilities of urban areas, the gathering crisis of ecology (so incapable of being handled by the traditional expansion of the marketplace), the growing blue-collar rebellion at the loss of significant work, the perceived inability of government to handle with well-focused institutional attention the common problems of the common life rather than the special problems and advantages of organized interest groups —all this signals a basic fault in the operation of American social reality, and the justifications of that reality in current interpretations of man. American politics has had no way of handling the politics of the common good because it is so fundamentally a polity of organized interest groups and marketplace tradeoffs. Interest-group pluralism may have served us well during the period of our national expansion, but its hope grows hopeless under the new conditions of our species survival.

It is here that our third criticism enters: the growing inability of religious realism adequately to console and so fund life with man's passion and care. The solace for the indeterminate ambiguities of human behavior "at the end of time" depends upon a view of the world as an inexhaustible and open-ended space for man's ever expanding vitalities, a taken-for-granted and automatic life-space. But now it is the human experiment itself, together with its natural life-support systems, that is viewed as

increasingly problematic. The marketplace can no longer take its
arena for granted. The expropriator of the world is coming face
to face with the possible expropriation of himself as a species. It
was one thing to have a tragic sense of reality and of the limits of
human virtue. It is quite another to experience the absurdity of
the vision of the human species collectively running over a cliff.
Belief in a divine completion "at the end of history" and an
afterlife for forgiven selves no longer provides the psychic poise
of earlier times.

In an age when man begins to see himself as seen and so
receive himself in reality as an earth creature in a galaxy of a
billion other sun systems, in a perceived universe of hundreds of
billions of such galaxies—under these conditions of species self-
definition, traditional religious realism cannot adequately provide
a dike against a growing feeling of cosmic relativization, a kind
of species humiliation and an ensuring sense of edgy bewilder-
ment, or perhaps determined indifference. We simply appear to
ourselves now as more alone, and in our aloneness more finally
responsible for our species experiment than we did under the
older reassurances. What we need is a reconstructed vision of
solace that will enable us to walk forward with steadiness, with
courage and care for mankind, even if it should happen that this
walk carry us in common loyalty over a common species cliff; yet
without resigning us to this perspective or to some hoped-for inter-
vention beyond man's full and final responsibility for his species
experiment.

It was this fundamental impasse in the evolution of our culture
which, I think, grasped the Harrisburg defendants. Their Catholic background helped them in this regard. Its greater confidence
in man's rationality and potential for community prepared them
for the hard discipline of hope. It preserved them from that loss
of public energy, that turning inward, which accompanies an
unrelieved fascination with man's corruptions. Moreover,
Catholicism has traditionally greeted with suspicion the scene of
unfettered ambitions that liberal individualism seemed to legitimate. "Commonweal" has been the touchstone of Catholic public

morality—that and a peculiarly unmodern seriousness of conscience (some have called it moralism) which refuses to console
itself short of dealing strictly with its internal normative demands. In these respects, Catholic traditionalism has offered a
better preparation for the human tasks of the latter half of the
twentieth century than that religious (or secular) realism which
to this day so influences the public ethos of our culture.

A NEW SENSE OF COMMONWEAL

Curiously, those who by heritage and by training have been
conditioned to a premodern view of man are better able to
register our passage into a post-modern human condition than
more uncomplicatedly "modern" men. For we begin to move into
a situation now where expansion of power and industry no longer
means an automatic advantage in the struggle to survive, a situation in which life increasingly requires balance and restraint. Put
simply, "winners" die too—in fact hasten the death of the rest of
us. Rather, our survival calls for a renewed sense of the organic
and of the interdependent, the connectedness of life: man to man
and man to earth. There is a closing in of the horizon, a perspective of limit rather than limitless expansion, a planet and a
species needing to settle down with each other. In a word, the
objective conditions of life are becoming again more "medieval."

Take for example the question of planning the public realm as
a common life-space, a "common good" without which all other
goods pass into oblivion. It was after all Thomas Aquinas who
argued that, "since therefore each man is a part of the city, it is
impossible that any man should be good unless he is well propor-
tioned to the common good."[13] That each man is "a part of the
city" bespeaks that classical and communal sense of reality which
simply got washed under in the volcanic rise of liberal, marketplace society. The English conservative Edmund Burke found
little to congratulate man on in this victory of the modern over
the medieval. He spoke instead for a lost sense of "reverence" for

society, a lost sense of gratitude for our common life, because, as he says,

> it is not a partnership in things subservient only to the gross animal existence of a temporary and perishable nature. It is a partnership in all science; a partnership in all art; a partnership in every virtue, and in all perfection. As the end of such a partnership cannot be obtained in many generations, it becomes a partnership not only between those who are living, but between those who are living, those who are dead, and those who are to be born (*Reflections on the Revolution in France*).

This classical and medieval sense of reality has traditionally been taught to Catholic seminarians in America. This means that the Catholicism of the Harrisburg defendants located them rather strategically in terms of grasping the necessities of man's existence today. It represents a reading of the social world where to be "respectable" means something more than running well the race of the self-made man. Society, far from being an automatic mechanism, is founded both in human intelligence and in man's fundamental sociality. It is subject therefore to inherent moral norms. There are acts which the marketplace may not deter, may even reward, but that are nevertheless morally illegitimate, inherently dishonorable.

All this parallels the returning sense that under the conditions of species survival, power needs other restraints besides other power, that the marketplace does not so much balance as expand the arena of conflict, and that whether the issue be violence abroad or distributive justice at home, human ambitions need the discipline of normative moral restraints. We can see this in the renewed attempt by legal and political scholars to delineate rationally defensible norms of the good society. It represents an unanticipated convergence of the medieval and the fully self-conscious contemporary mind. Which is to say that however admittedly stumbling in their politics and naive in their moral enthusiasm, the world of the Harrisburg defendants may be less unrealistic than the increasingly unreal world of the older realists.

To sum up, the Berrigan conspiracy trial can be viewed in its wider cultural context as a scene of contending legitimacies. Liberal individualism's power-marketplace view of society provides the context by which to weave together disparate pieces of the indictment and of the trial, and shows the connection of Harrisburg to more recent political events such as Watergate. The Catholic traditionalism of the defendants set them apart from the consolations of religious realism which to this day corners the market on sophisticated solace. It provided them critical distance for the task of modern survival.

Finally, I am persuaded that none of these things are going to leave us alone, that simply to put the Harrisburg trial behind is to fail to grasp the trial we all face ahead. Our attempt to understand it is not so much a memory as a preparation.

NOTES

1. I am grateful to Garry Wills for drawing my attention to this quote. See his *Bare Ruined Choirs* (New York: Doubleday, 1972), p. 141.

2. *Ideology and Utopia* (New York: Harvest, 1936), p. 22.

3. "Legitimacy in the Modern State," in *Power and Community*, eds. Green and Levinson (New York: Pantheon, 1969), p. 313.

4. *Obligations: Essays on Disobedience, War, and Citizenship* (Boston: Harvard University Press, 1970), p. 113.

5. Wills, *Nixon Agonistes* (Boston: Houghton Mifflin, 1970), pp. 585, 594.

6. *The Wealth of Nations*, Bk. IV, ch. 7.

7. *The End of Liberalism* (New York: Norton, 1969), p. 97.

8. Quoted in the *New York Times*, July 12, 1973, p. 25.

9. See "Lying in Politic, Reflections on the Pentagon Papers," in *Crises of the Republic* (New York: Harcourt Brace Jovanovich, 1972).

10. Published in *Win* magazine, March 1972.

11. *The Nature and Destiny of Man* (New York: Scribner's, 1949), p. 181.

12. *Children of Light and Children of Darkness* (New York: Scribner's, 1950), p. 189.

13. *Summa Theologica* I–II, q. 92, a.1.